WOMEN IN THE CITY OF THE DEAD

The 'City of the Dead' is a vast and ancient cemetery close to the centre of Cairo which has gradually become a permanent home for thousands of migrants from the countryside. For many of the women, though still living in poverty, migration has brought a change of role. The demands of men are still the determinant force, but the women, in their new non-traditional setting, have a much greater control over their own lives, as the exclusively female gatherings which form the setting for this book clearly show.

Helen Watson, a Fellow in Anthropology at St. John's College, Cambridge, has spent long periods inside this world, where autobiographical narration and fictional story-telling are routine social pastimes. She transcribes the stories and introduces the tellers and their society.

Women in the City of the Dead

Helen Watson

Africa World Press, Inc.

P.O. Box 1892
Trenton, NJ 08607

P.O. Box 48
Asmara, ERITREA

Africa World Press, Inc.

P.O. Box 1892
Trenton, NJ 08607

P.O. Box 48
Asmara, ERITREA

Library of Congress Catalog Card No: 91-76981

ISBN: 0-86543-280-5 *Cloth*
       0-86543-281-3 *Paper*

PREFACE

There is romance and revelation in the telling of tales. The romance is for everyone, the revelation is for those willing or able to perceive it. What is essential to all storytelling is that the ordinary and the extraordinary are interwoven into a rich tapestry which represents an alternative view of everyday life. Storytellers are attracted to the fantastic, they spin a complex web of symbols and half-hidden references which hangs over the surface of the tale. The transformation takes place when a veil is draped over mundane lives and familiar emotions, and the impact on an intimate audience is mesmerising. Tales divert, warn, redeem, entertain and justify. Everyone has a story and is willing to tell it.

When women meet in the evenings, everyone seems to be talking at once but all ears are tuned in to the flow of conversation, listening for a sign that a tale is to be told. Customary modesty and demure attitudes get lost in the telling of tales. Bawdy, gaudy images spice each story as a matter of course. Among themselves, behind closed shutters, women can say what they want.

The tales from *One Thousand and One Arabian Nights* spring to mind. The women's tales also defy categorisation; a rich mixture of folk tale, fable, fairy story and personal anecdote. Storytellers give lessons in moral philosophy, they transport mere mortals into the spirit world and conjure up lives full of coincidence and surprise. Ordinary people are made to suffer common trials and tribulations in an exotic world where their ultimate fate parallels their inner nature and external experiences.

ACKNOWLEDGEMENTS

To the late John Blacking for his inspiration.

Thanks also to Ernest Gellner for encouragement and to numerous friends and colleagues for their creative input, especially to Nadia and Laila for patient linguistic advice and to Gaby for comments on an early draft. Particular thanks to Dai for listening to each tale as it emerged in its present form, sole member of a reduced, but critical storytelling circle.

CONTENTS

MAPS & ILLUSTRATIONS

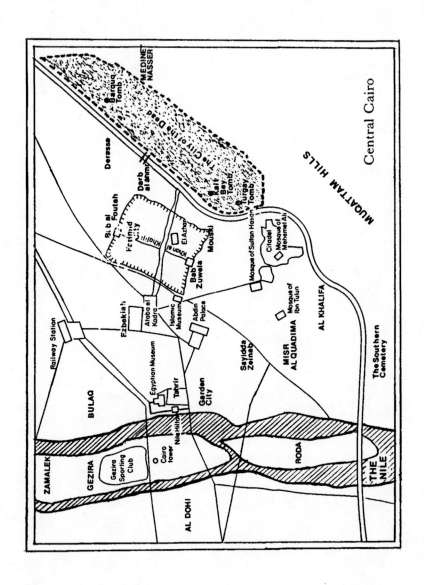

Central Cairo

MUQATTAM HILLS

MEDINET NASSER

Barqua Tomb

Derassa

The City of the Dead

Kait Bey Tomb

Turgay

Darb al Ahmar

Bib al Foutah

Fetimid City

Khan al Kholili

El Azhar

Mouski

Bab Zuwela

Mosque of Sultan Hasan Tomb

Citadel

Mosque of Mehemel Ali

Ezbekia'h

Ataba el Kadra

Islamic Museum

Abdin Palace

Mosque of Ibn Tulun

AL KHALIFA

MISR AL QUADIMA

Seyidda Zeinab

Railway Station

Egyptian Museum

Tahrir

Garden City

Nile Hilton

The Southern Cemetery

ZAMALEK

GEZIRA

Gezira Sporting Club

Cairo Tower

BULAQ

AL DOHI

RODA

THE NILE

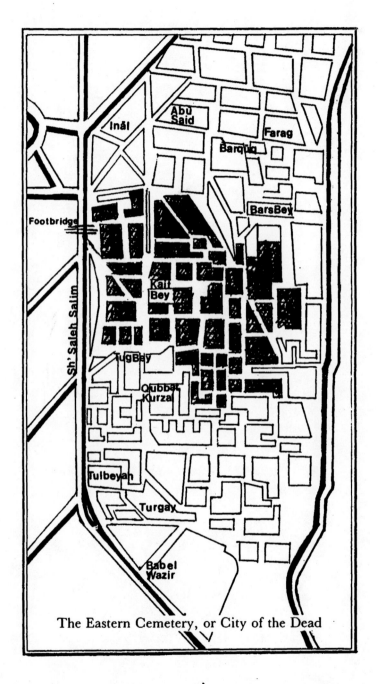

The Eastern Cemetery, or City of the Dead

INTRODUCTORY

This book, *One Thousand and One Nights*, abounds with splendid biographies that teach the reader to detect deception and to protect himself from it, as well as delighting and diverting him whenever he is burdened with the cares of life and the ills of the world [. . .]

Shahrazad said, 'If you wish I can tell you many tales. In the end if you don't take me to King Shahrayar I shall go to him myself behind your back and tell him that you have begrudged your master one like me.' The vizier asked, 'Must you really do this?' She replied, 'Yes I must.' [. . .]

Shahrazad went to her younger sister Dinarazad and said, 'Listen well to what I am telling you. When I go to the king I will send for you and when you see that the king has finished with me say, "Sister if you are not sleepy tell us a story." Then I will begin to tell a story and it will cause the king to stop his practice, save myself and deliver the people.' [. . .]

Shahrazad turned to King Shahrayar and said, 'May I have your permission to tell a tale?' He replied, 'Yes' and Shahrazad was very happy and said, 'Listen!'

— *The Arabian Nights*, translated by Husain Haddawy from the text edited by Muhsin Mahdi

THE CITY OF THE DEAD

The Local Social World

The life stories and tales in this book were told by women who live in the City of the Dead in Cairo. The City of the Dead is a graveyard more than four centuries old, which stretches for over three kilometres along one of the main roads into and out of the city. It is in fact made up of four cemeteries which have merged and are now practically indistinguishable from each other. The oldest parts date from the era of Egypt's Mameluk rulers. Sultan Farag erected a tomb for his father Barquq in the early fifteenth century, and the City of the Dead (also known as the Eastern Cemetery) became a popular burial place for later emirs and sultans. Few of the original tombs and burial vaults remain and most enclosures date from the eighteenth and nineteenth centuries. Most of the much earlier Turkish and Mameluk tombs have fallen into ruin and disappeared, or were demolished to make space for new buildings.

Behind a great wall, bounded on both sides by a busy multi-lane motorway, the City of the Dead appears a deserted relic of past times, cut off from the modern city and the densely populated urban districts nearby. The flow of passing traffic is constant, in one direction to the suburbs and the airport, in the other to the Citadel and old Cairo. The casual observer may not notice this walled-in wasteland and may even dismiss it as another of Cairo's building sites. Viewed from a distance the necropolis looks like an ancient, rather elaborate model village where box-shaped buildings have been set out along grid lines in a random sequence. There are wide avenues separating major tombs in the oldest areas, which make the buildings seem smaller and give an impression of the space and grandeur of a former era.

The City of the Dead has been inhabited for several centuries, originally by guardians of the tombs and old family retainers. In more recent times the number of inhabitants has increased dramatically, a consequence of several interlinked factors: city-ward migration, external pressures in surrounding areas and Cairo's overpopulation and chronic housing shortage. Grand old tombs and rough newly-built dwellings are clustered together in parts of the City of the Dead, forming distinct close-knit neighbourhoods. In most places the living now outnumber the dead.

Many of the inhabitants were born far from Cairo in Egypt's agricultural or desert regions. Most harbour the dream of returning to their area of origin, but few have the means to do so. Families from diverse regions and backgrounds live side by side, but there is a very strong sense of community and inter-dependence. People have developed a united front against everyday hardship, aware that their common condition over-rides anything that might divide them.

Moving into the city has forced most local migrants into a position of extreme hardship. Living conditions are poor. Families have moved into tomb buildings and ceremonial ante-rooms, and additional dwellings and extensions have been tacked on as required. Basic facilities are either self-assembled and dangerously inadequate, or simply do not exist. A less obvious but equally serious difficulty is the migrants' emotional burden of separation from their rural homeland and village kin. 'The Village' is an ever-present subject of conversation, and people discuss the lifestyle and values of their rural ancestors with an unmistakable sense of longing and romance. Many are trapped in the city, having sold their land and lost contact with their home area. Most cannot afford a return fare let alone the cost of a new farm. People must learn to live with the realisation of poor migrants everywhere: city streets are rarely paved with gold.

There is a lot of pride at stake in objective evaluation of the facts and few men would admit that they are worse off as a result of migration. In any case there is little point in such thoughts when there is no chance to undo the damage or recoup their losses. As a result people have a seemingly unshakable optimism and direct their hopes to a future when things are bound to improve. Another important compensation for present hardship is fervent belief in divine providence and the omniscient, omnipotent will of Allah. This is coupled with an awareness of the futility of complaint. A theme of many well loved folk songs is the misery of the uprooted peasant whose need of sympathy is expressed with deep sorrow and understanding. One song asks the question which is on many people's lips: 'To whom shall I complain when all are suffering injustice?'

I came to know the people of one neighbourhood in the City of the Dead very well when I was carrying out anthropological research in Cairo into women's experience of migration and the effect of urban life on family relationships, and I had the kind of good fortune anthropologists depend on in a foreign and quite alien culture. People were hospitable, patient and prepared to put up with my persistent questions. The initial focus of my research was women's contribution to the family budget and their experience of waged work. Many women had been forced to earn money for the first time as a direct result of migration. Rural women undertake many types of farm work, but this is unpaid and considered an acceptable and obligatory part of their duty as family members. Waged work to supplement family income in the city is viewed quite differently and is the cause of a number of crucial conflicts for women and their families.

The Women's Social World

In Arab-Muslim society there is a complex, well defined and highly structured set of gender roles which underpins personal and public life and gives marriage and the family a central importance. In the City of the Dead this is evident in many overt aspects of everyday social life which outsiders usually associate with the Arab-Muslim world in general. Women and men do not mix freely. Women keep at a distance from men as much as possible and dress in the familiar body-concealing clothes, while men crowd the coffee houses and public places. There are few women who appear at ease in the streets. A high value is placed on female modesty, and this explains many of the restrictions on women's freedom of movement, conduct, style of dress and so on. Female virginity is the *sine qua non* of marriage, and marriage itself is a universal goal. On these two counts alone it is vital for a woman to avoid any charge of immodest behaviour, since this would impair her marriage prospects.

Despite how it might appear to an outsider, this is not a system which is imposed on women in any obvious sense of the word. The segregation of the sexes and observance of a strict code of conduct is valued and actively maintained by women themselves. An ideal female way of life is popularly expressed in terms of the cloistered seclusion women enjoyed in the past. Secluded quarters and confinement are no longer possible, although women know of a few rural elites who can afford to keep their female kin in seclusion and do without their labour in the fields. This is discussed with a candid and clear envy, since the women's own families relied heavily on their agricultural work before migration. The equivalent urban image of a secluded lifestyle is that of a rich businessman's wife who never leaves her luxurious home and spends all day watching television after ordering groceries by telephone. Conscious that the lifestyle they desire is denied to them by poverty, local women's positive view of seclusion is dominated by the idea of liberation from financial problems and hard unfulfilling work.

For the women like this who most desire it, total sexual segregation is an unlikely prospect because of overcrowded living conditions, in the City of the Dead as in many urban centres of the Arab-Muslim world. But the values and norms which govern such a lifestyle remain intact and are a strong influence on behaviour and attitudes. Moreover, the impact of western-facing and urban values is equally weak in the City of the Dead. Modernity has very little effect on how women live, or indeed on how they want to live. Familiar western concepts of sexual equality and the liberation of women are irrelevant and unnecessary from local women's point of view. At the core of this conviction is the perception that gender roles and male and female responsibilities are fully complementary. There is a male sphere of influence and activity and a female one; both are separate and distinct, but in combination they form the basis of a stable society.

These ideas are most obvious in women's view of work. Waged work is an essential part of men's social duty. Men are the breadwinners, family provisioners and protectors. At his marriage every man takes his wife from her father's care and protection and assumes the father's complete responsibility for her welfare and material comfort. The male realm is outside the home, even if inevitably focused towards it. This is the public world which involves work, money and looking after family affairs. The women's realm is the home. Motherhood, child

care, cooking, cleaning and managing domestic affairs make up
the primary female sphere of influence and activity.

Conflict and change tend to have a catastrophic effect on any
highly structured system. Women's increasing presence in the
male world of work and money provides great potential for
disruption of the complementary nature of male and female
roles. This is a cause of considerable concern to both men and
women.

Women view waged work as a necessary evil. They have to
earn money to help feed the family but they fear that it interferes
with their 'real work' of managing domestic affairs and looking
after children. All women emphasise that their home life
remains the first priority. However much time they spend earning money, it is not at the expense of a well organised house and
the welfare of children. Inevitably, women carry the double
burden of two workloads. The situation is made more difficult
by male attitudes to women's work. Men's ability to provide for
family needs is undermined by low wages and poor economic
prospects, which are a major source of personal shame. The fact
that most men have to rely on their wives' incomes compounds
such feelings of inadequacy. Women, in turn, are profoundly
affected by this and have to come to terms with the shame their
income represents in male eyes. At the same time they have to
ensure that their job and the work it entails are judged acceptable by local standards of female modesty. In many respects
women face an impossible dilemma.

A common solution to resolve the obvious aspects of the problem is home-based employment. Most women work at home
in badly paid sewing and petty manufacturing jobs. The main
advantages are that the work is hidden from public view, and
they can juggle the time they spend on the job with the time they
spend on domestic duties and child care. For many women the
crucial factor is that they work behind closed doors.

Economic considerations remain largely secondary, even for
the very poorest women, although the higher wages of a factory
job would certainly reduce the hardship faced by all families in
the neighbourhood. This provides some sense of the high value
of domestic life for women and the strength of the boundaries
separating the male and the female worlds. While women manage some of the problems entailed in employment by choosing

a job which minimises the risk of conflict with the established social order, on a practical level women's solidarity and mutual reliance help to reduce their double burden of waged work and housekeeping.

Marriage is an important source of security and solidarity for women, albeit by an indirect and complicated route. Although it is easy to think of marriage as a series of economic or self-interested agreements between men, women's role in match-making tends to give them a considerable, if informal, control over arranged marriages behind the scenes. Women trade in local gossip, and vital information about prospective spouses flows through these all-female channels of communication long before men of the household are aware of it. Information is a powerful tool in such circumstances; marriage plans either advance or collapse when women withhold or manipulate certain facts about the families concerned. A likely candidate might not come to the attention of the father of a prospective spouse because his wife, convinced that he or she is unsuitable, has already eliminated that person from the final line-up.

Although women's part in the matchmaking process is subtle and concealed (and often devious), it is the only way open to them to plan a marriage which secures their own interests. A young woman may appear to have very little say in the choice of her own husband, but her mother, sisters and maternal aunts usually combine forces to find her a man well known to them, and one who is often the son of a close female friend. When maternal relatives marry, it further expands and strengthens women's mutual support groups, since blood ties are being cemented by marriage. In such cases the female members of both families have long-established relationships which transcend the marriage itself. It is not surprising that local men have a very low opinion of this type of marriage. They stress its flaws from a husband's point of view: 'Too many women with too many things to keep them interested in themselves' was how one man put it. But just as predictable, given women's manipulation of marriage arrangements, is that this type of marriage is common and its advantages are a frequent topic of discussion among women.

Local women are tough, resourceful and mutually self-reliant. They depend on each other for assistance in their work and domestic life.

There is always a pool of female labour prepared to find the time to take care of sick children and provide extra support in an emergency. Female friendship involves very strong and intimate bonds. Among women there is always a sense that they only have each other to rely on against the vagaries of a harsh world and the unpredictability of men. Devotion to children unites all women as mothers or soon-to-be mothers, and children are every woman's personal and social mainstay. Sons are a source of security for old women and every mother is well aware that a grown-up son will return the care she has lavished on him. Women derive most of their personal and social worth from motherhood. A woman judges herself (and is judged) by the number of children she bears. 'She was a fine woman, the mother of many sons' is a standard compliment.

The insecurity and hardship of daily life might suggest that depression and misery characterise the local social world. On the contrary, people are cheerful and determined to make the best of things. Women, even more than men, are determined to meet every problem head on and refuse to give way to despair when faced with what might seem an impossible problem. Although the conflicts inherent in a changing society and culture are a serious threat to social stability, women hold family and social life together by masking signs of change that they feel are undesirable or dangerous. From their perspective there is little point in exacerbating potential sources of conflict in an already insecure world. Working women choose to conceal their jobs from their husbands and so help them to save face. Those who work to support their family in a man's absence justify their despised employment as an extension of their duty as a mother. In this way old norms and values persist in a new environment, but in the process they are being adapted to the new world.

A way of life which might be called traditional is subject to change and decay in the city, but it continues to have meaning and importance to men and women alike. Women interpret and respond to the changing world according to the roles and ideals they value most: motherhood, wifehood and female friendship. In this way they maintain the close-knit bonds of the women's world and create the means to cope with everyday problems of scarcity, uprootedness and isolation.

My aim in this book is to let the women speak for themselves. The personal experiences related in the life histories give an impression of women's view of the world. I recorded the life histories during my time in the City of the Dead as we worked together, chatted, fed children and cooked family dinners. On these occasions I felt less like an anthropologist than a modern-day scribe and confessor. As my collection of tape recordings grew it rivalled my academic notes on patterns of migration and marriage. The more I became involved in the lives of local women, at times I felt torn between my original research project and the insights I gleaned from women's accounts of everyday life. The life histories and tales had to be set aside on return to university and the analysis of facts and figures accumulated during fieldwork, but it was impossible to forget them. Being able to share something of these women's lives was a pleasure, a privilege and a memorable experience. Even now in my own quite different social world, it is not difficult to recollect each of the women through the force of their words.

The task of translating and recreating the narratives was dominated by considerations of form, content and style. A major concern was how best to transfer the spoken word to the printed page. Given the gulf which separates the written and the spoken, I tried to find a literary bridge between the words the women chose and the conventions of print. My approach has been to construct a framework for the narratives which gives the reader a sense of being present as the tales are told. In translating from the original Arabic my aim was to capture the rhythms and imagery employed in the telling of tales, and to convey the common themes as well as the range of creative imagination at work by presenting the tales and life histories as a series of interrelated narratives. Nevertheless there is the constant fear that in writing down what was spoken and retelling the stories and tales in English, some of the richness and spontaneity of the women's words may be lost. If my part in the story-telling process has involved some compromise, my hope is that it is not at the expense of the dramatic essence of women's accounts of their own experiences.

One day when I was making laborious research notes a woman said, 'Words from the heart are more alive than your scribblings. When we speak, our words burn. Do yours?' The answer to that question must lie in the following attempt to recreate the spirit of their words.

THE WOMEN AND THE TALES

The Storytelling Circle

A group of women meet most evenings and spend a relaxed, informal hour or two together before·the men of the household return for dinner. Conversation is loud and lively, and ten to twelve voices generate more noise than might be assumed possible. Tea, cakes and sweets are served once everyoꞏe has arrived and the hostess keeps a conscientious eye on the state of supplies throughout the evening. The atmosphere is warm and intimate. Sometimes it is not unlike a Victorian lady's At Home day dominated by tea-soaked gossip. At other times it is more like a teenage birthday party when giggles at a rude joke infect subsequent events. High spirits and revelry have a cumulative, infectious effect on most occasions.

Three women arrange to act as hostess on an informal basis. Each has a tiny back room not in constant use by other family members which is ideally suited for entertaining female friends in relative seclusion. These rooms have a heavy curtain which is drawn to create an impression of privacy and makes the room seem like a twilight retreat from the busy world outside. Prying eyes cannot penetrate the curtain and men would not dream of entering, although they make their presence known in other ways without reservation and interrupt women's gatherings as a matter of course.

The hostesses are familiar important figures in the neighbourhood, they can be described as the senior women of the community and command respect from everyone. Their mature age and high status go a long way towards defusing any criticism men might want to make about their wives attending the gatherings. When women meet to chat and gossip men tend to think of it as frivolous time-wasting, although these gatherings have the same basic purpose as men's visits to a coffee house — a chance to relax away from the family in the company of friends and neighbours.

There is no formal structure or set rule of conduct to govern the gatherings, other than that the women tend to arrive at a certain agreed time in the late afternoon and depart before nightfall, around eight. Everyone finds a place to sit on plump floor cushions in the tiny room, where lack of space makes it inevitable that each woman sits shoulder to shoulder with her neighbour. The babies and young children brought by their mothers soon fill any gaps in the already crowded room. It becomes even more cramped and noisy when children are distributed among the guests, and most laps are occupied by at least one child.

The women swap news and gossip much as they do whenever and wherever they meet, but, unlike doorstep encounters and communal laundry sessions at the water-pump, conversation among women in the curtained-off room is much more informal, unbridled and candid. The basic facts about an impending marriage may filter through the community by many different female-controlled channels, but piquant details and 'off the record' remarks are reserved for a select audience of close friends at all-female get-togethers. The women may dismiss the quality of a bride-to-be's trousseau, then apply the same sharp tongue to the girl's face and figure. The most bawdy and vicious comments tend to be reserved for speculation about the bedroom charms of prospective grooms. One handsome young man would have been deeply embarrassed on the eve of his wedding party had he known that his aunt's neighbours were revealing how they had cured his bed-wetting by making him wear a sand-filled nappy. Someone suggested that his new wife should be advised to do likewise 'in case the old problem returned'.

While local news and views form an important and highly significant part of the social content of gatherings, storytelling is regarded as the highlight of an evening together. Women often explained that a tale was the perfect end to an entertaining evening. There is no strict boundary to mark where general conversation ends and a tale begins. Indeed the women occasionally get caught up in the intricacies and intrigues of some new neighbourhood scandal and the discussion lasts all evening, leaving no time for a tale at all. But on most evenings someone will call for a tale in a lull in the conversation. There are no strings attached in so far as the style of the tale or the person of the storyteller is concerned; a woman simply asks for a tale as if reminding everyone that a tale is good entertainment at this point of the evening. The suggestion is always seconded by an enthusiastic chorus of agreement until a storyteller obliges.

The women are granted their wish when one of the company announces that she will tell a tale. The offer is made with a casual phrase like 'I'll tell a tale if you want' or 'I have a tale if you'll listen'.

Anyone may tell a tale, although in practice the hostess and another of the older women do so most frequently. These women are considered to be the best storytellers and they tell most of the tales. The storytellers' knowledge of community affairs gives them a wealth of personal details about women's lives, which can be woven into a tale. They know the circumstances behind any scandal, success or tragedy as well as every local birth, marriage or death. Their in-depth information is often gathered through close involvement in key events in other women's lives in the capacity of midwife, matchmaker or mourner. The facts are usually known within the community as a whole, but in less detail, and such things are rarely mentioned since they concern sensitive and painful experiences. A close female friend is even likely to feign ignorance and surprise when someone refers to one of these taboo aspects of her life, although both sides are aware that the revelation and response are part of a social charade. Gossips will chronicle a neighbour's personal affairs but no hint of the intimate knowledge they possess is shown in face to face encounters. The boundary between personal and intimate exchanges is absolute and never broken in normal circumstances.

In tales it is a quite different matter. Storytelling is a highly-charged emotional activity which pays little heed to open wounds inflicted by real life. Storytellers are not bound by the rules of polite society and conversation and their tales are expected to be provocative, evocative and exciting. They must stir the members of the audience and touch raw nerves. The portmanteau of sensitive information at a storyteller's disposal is opened indiscriminately and used to flavour her tales with subtle, yet penetrating references to other women present.

As soon as a storyteller identifies herself the level of noise in the room falls sharply and everyone gives the speaker full attention. Although the background chatter ceases when a tale begins, there is nothing akin to respectful silence while it is being told. On the contrary, audience participation is expected and delivered with gusto. The women sigh, gasp, exclaim, roar with laughter and make ironical or witty responses to rhetorical questions. At times the atmosphere is reminiscent of a controversial debate among politicians. But however rowdy the evening might be, it is unthinkable for a storyteller not to finish a tale she has started, and the narrative's flow is never interrupted in a way that might prove fatal. A tale was halted on just one occasion when it provoked a very emotional response from one of the women present, but it was resumed within a few minutes when the interrupter calmed down. Although everyone was sympathetic and comforted the distressed woman, they acted as if her outburst was shocking for reasons other than her obvious upset, and there was a sense that she had transgressed some unwritten code by bringing the tale to a sudden halt. The circumstances of that peculiar evening are important for a number of reasons which will be related in the context of the woman's life story and the tale itself, where they have most resonance.

At the end of a tale the women have another round of tea drinking unless it is already late and they have to get back to the kitchen to serve the family meal. There is much that even a casual observer can glean from women's reactions at the end of the evening. If a tragic tale has been told the women may be subdued, as if they will carry the warnings of the tale home with them. If there has been a comic tale full of in-jokes and barbed comments, women repeat the jokes and remind each other of the funniest parts as they leave the house. On many evenings one of the most striking aspects of the leave-taking is the depth of a particular woman's response to the tale which has been told. While this is difficult to describe in general terms (and of course everyone reacts differently to different tales), some mention of basic features is necessary to preface the examples included in this collection of life histories and tales.

From time to time a woman might react to a tale in some dramatic and memorable fashion which marks her behaviour as different from that of other members of the audience. If most women wept after a sad tale or laughed at a farcical one, someone else might have appeared too stunned to weep or too embarrassed to laugh with the rest of the company. My growing awareness of such unusually profound reactions eventually led me to wonder if a particular tale had some hidden personal significance for an individual present in the room.

Seven women had allowed me to record detailed life histories and there seemed to be numerous echoes of real-life experiences in the tales I was hearing in the storytelling circle. There seemed to be a direct link between events in the women's lives and the tales they listened to, and I began to recognise that certain tales could be associated with the women I knew. Sometimes there was such a neat fit between the plot of a tale and events related in a life history that the relationship was immediately obvious. At other times it only became apparent at the end of the tale or, later still, when I followed up a particular detail from one of the life histories and was suddenly reminded of a tale. Of course in retrospect it is clear that each woman's response to what I came to call 'her tale' confirmed the relationship between them at the time. I hope this happens with each of the narratives in much the same way it did when I listened to the women describe their lives and heard the storytellers tell their tales.

The Women

AMIRA is the key-stone of the women's circle, not that this is immediately obvious. She is quiet and reserved and shuns the social limelight. She is well known and loved for her reliability and generosity. Everyone turns to Amira in difficult situations and she always finds time to help. If the cupboard is empty and unexpected guests arrive, Amira is a dependable source of emergency food supplies. If children are sick and a woman has to work, Amira is a ready and willing child-minder. One neighbour distilled local women's view of Amira thus: 'Amira always saves the day. However impossible the problem, Amira will help sort it out.' However, despite her popularity and the respect she is accorded, Amira remains an outsider within the social world of women. She has lived alone for most of her adult life since a divorce and public accusation of infertility. The fact that she has no children sets her apart from other women in this community where female status is inextricably linked to motherhood. Amira considers that she is cursed and less than human because of her childlessness and she compensates for this by living to help others.

OUM IDRIS is one of the liveliest women in the group, always outspoken and opinionated. Her life has been a series of controversial and colourful events and she derives a measured degree of self-importance from this. Although Oum Idris is well liked because she has a great sense of irreverent fun and enjoys deflating pompous and pious egos, her socially-questionable past means that she is not quite respectable. For many years she was possessed by a spirit which made her behave in unseemly ways and neglect her domestic duties. The spirit was eventually exorcised and Oum Idris relates that her 'true character' emerged after this when she became a 'model mother'. Another major scandal surrounding Oum Idris concerns her son, Idris the 'deviant' as he used to be known, a former petty criminal and local miscreant. To her great delight he appears to have reformed since he married a woman with an equally blemished reputation. Oum Idris is a matchmaker of consummate skill, as is clear from her son's marriage. She delights in sizing up potential couples and plays a leading role in deliberations over 'ideal' spouses. Oum Idris is convinced that the most important facet of her character is determination. She cites her experiences as proof that everyone has the capacity to alter the course of his or her life and forget the errors of the past.

OUM MOHAMMED is the oldest woman in the neighbourhood and a highly respected member of the community. She enjoys being the centre of social occasions and is the supreme hostess of many women's gatherings. She likes to make fun of the formal courtesies directed towards her, but she commands respect and can be awesome in her anger if she feels slighted or overlooked. Her three marriages and two divorces make her a self-proclaimed expert on the stupidity of husbands, the strength of wives and the joys of motherhood. She has given birth to more than twenty children and her experiences illustrate the potential advantages and drawbacks of matriarchy. Oum Mohammed relishes the company of younger women and her acquired role as adviser and counsellor. She is especially eager to draw attention to her own triumphs over weak men and to encourage other women to follow her example. Her wealth of experience encapsulates some of the greatest hardships women may have to face, from being deserted and divorced, to life as a street trader, to victim of the Evil Eye. She herself eventually found happiness with a 'good man' and her large family is a source of great pride. Oum Mohammed attributes her success in life to stubborn resourcefulness and an ability to 'outwit any man'.

OUM ALI is one of the most nervous and fearful women of the group. She is profoundly pessimistic and fatalistic. She considers that her life has been one long series of disasters and crises. Other women are sympathetic for the most part, but local gossip tends to characterise her as somewhat self-obsessed and melodramatic. She complains about her problems incessantly and most of her friends, who have considerable troubles of their own, find this irritating. Oum Ali is very proud of her prestigious rural ancestry, although she feels that a down-turn in family fortunes marked the beginning of her own tragic decline. Although Oum Ali's pessimism and bitter complaints are often a source of annoyance, she has some justification for this outlook, having experienced a great many sad and difficult circumstances in just thirty years. Oum Ali's father lost his land and she had to marry into a poor family. Her husband then brought her to the city but failed to achieve any material benefits from migration. Her first two sons died shortly after birth and she considers her daughter to be neglectful and disrespectful. A third son who survived is sickly and a cause of constant worry. Finally, she was widowed after five years of this unhappy marriage. At this stage in her life, Oum Ali says that she lives in expectation of the next, inevitable disaster.

OUM KARIM appears to be much older than her twenty-four years. She is perpetually worn out by the double burden of work and caring for her young family. She is ashamed of the fact that she has to work to supplement her husband's earnings and tries to keep this hidden from him to counteract his feelings of inadequacy: Oum Karim is conscious that her husband considers himself 'less of a man' because he cannot fulfil his duty as family breadwinner. She is a devoted mother and the children are her main source of comfort and happiness. She invests all her energy in caring for the children, although she fights with constant feelings of guilt that her work causes her to neglect them. She works at home cutting out garments for a local dressmaker, and although this is particularly suited to her domestic situation, wages are low and a great deal of work is required to earn the small sum of money she needs. Amira, a very close friend and confidante, often looks after Oum Karim's children when the dressmaker overloads her with orders. This is a great comfort to Oum Karim but she remains 'sick with guilt and fear' in case the children feel deprived of their mother's attention. Oum Karim's greatest hope is that her daughters will escape the cycle of poverty and want in which she herself is trapped, but she can see no alternative way of life for herself if the family is not to starve.

OUM SHERIF is the most recent member of the circle of friends. She is one of the younger women, about Oum Karim's age, and they share many of the same problems. She is particularly friendly with Oum Karim and Oum Ali, although she is popular with all the women, who are genuinely sorry for her. Oum Sherif and her husband arrived from a remote rural area less than three years ago and have not become well integrated into the community. She feels very homesick and isolated from her own kin because she has not been able to see them since her marriage and there is no way of contacting their village from the city. Her husband works in another district of the city and is away from home for most of the day. He forbids her to mix with local women, considering them improperly immodest and neglectful of the expected, appropriate code of female conduct. Oum Sherif's marriage has never been happy and her husband treats her very harshly, all the more so since the death of their son. She was very weak and malnourished after the birth and unable to feed the child. Her husband blamed her for the baby's death and their marriage rapidly deteriorated. Her greatest fear is divorce, because she has no family in the city and would be unable to provide for herself and her recent baby daughter. Despite all this, Oum Sherif thrives in the company of the small group of women and depends on Oum Mohammed and Amira for advice and help. She is gradually becoming aware of the support women are able to give each other and growing more confident about the future.

OUM MUSTAFA is a widow who had to learn how to provide for herself and her young sons after a long and happy marriage. She had lived in semi-seclusion for most of her adult life and had no experience of the outside world. Her husband's death brought this protected and deeply cherished way of life to an abrupt end. Oum Mustafa took over her husband's vegetable stall with the help of her more worldly-wise sister and has become a prosperous trader by local standards. She manages to feed her family and still save something towards the cost of her sons' education. Oum Mustafa exhibits a surprising degree of self-confidence and pride, given that she had little experience of the 'men's world of the streets' until late in life. She often pools resources with Oum Mohammed and other older, more finan-cially secure women to help Oum Karim and Oum Sherif, and she gives regular gifts of food to the children. Oum Mustafa's sense of pride in her achievements is easily understood, and she is well regarded as a woman who has learned self-reliance and independence in very difficult circumstances. However, occa-sional bouts of nostalgia for her perfect marriage and life of seclusion tend to be seen as tactless and to rankle among her friends, since few of the women have, or dream of having, first-hand experience of such a comfortable, leisurely lifestyle.

Each of these seven women, if asked, would describe herself as an ordinary member of an ordinary family. The women's every-day activities and interests revolve around ordinary concerns: husbands, children, making ends meet and making the most of life in a poor neighbourhood in Cairo. If the events and experiences the women describe make their lives seem tragic, dramatic and even extraordinary, this is not how the women think of the situation themselves. As an outsider who shared the same social world that these women inhabit, I must stress that their experiences are rarely exaggerated in that they are largely typical of those which dominate all women's daily existence in the City of the Dead. In the words of an often-heard simple state-ment of fact: life isn't easy for women around here.

The life histories are accounts of personal experiences and relationships which give an impression of the scope of all 'ordinary' women's lives. The tales may seem less straightfor-ward, but it should not be difficult to grasp their significance; as with a storyteller's audience, it is simply a matter of making connections based on shared knowledge and mutual under-standing of other women's lives.

An additional life history — that of Laila, who is not a member of the circle to which the other seven belong — is also included (see page 92, below).

The City of the Dead: panorama from the roof of Kait Bey mosque.

One of the 'district squares' in the City of the Dead: a centre of social and trading activity.

The City of the Dead viewed from the potters' quarter, with the fires of its rubbish dump rising in the background.

Two sisters, aged *ca.* 12 and 14, for whom marriages were being arranged at the time of the author's acquaintance with them; seen beside their uncle's loom.

An old woman looking after the child of her working daughter, washing at a street tap.

Secluded girls, and a boy who is free to roam but is being watched by them for his safety. The picture and inscription on the house wall record a previous owner's *haj* (pilgrimage to Mecca).

LIFE HISTORIES AND TALES

AMIRA: A CHILDLESS WOMAN

Amira is always one of the first to arrive each evening. She comes laden with small gifts of sweets which she has made as a contribution to the supper. She is also the last to leave, since she always helps the hostess tidy up when the other women have gone home. During the evening Amira's preferred place is next to the curtain which divides the women's room from the kitchen. She usually sits right at the back and rarely takes part in the chat and gossip unless someone asks her opinion. Apart from her self-appointed duties as the hostess's assistant, Amira's presence at the storytelling circle might go unnoticed. She is the only woman who never comments on a tale unless asked, and she rarely joins in the general noisy spirit of excitement during a tale. Although Amira makes little impression on the company and takes a backseat role in the evening's entertainment, she is always listening and watching intently. She watches the faces of other women and seems to be sizing up their responses to the tale. If a child starts to whimper or grow restless, Amira is usually the first to deal with this threat to the flow of a tale. The children are very comfortable in Amira's care, since they know her very well as a favourite child-minder. Amira seems happiest when she assumes responsibility for other women's children and is cradling their sleeping infants. She is usually surrounded by a cluster of children throughout the evening. Amira's great love of children is explained by the central theme of her life story.

I was born about fifty years ago, maybe a little more, I can't be sure. It was in a different part of Cairo, a district quite far from here near Giseh.* My father had come to

---

* Giseh (Giza) is a southern suburb of Cairo near the Pyramids. Amira's father is said to have lived in a settlement to the south-west of the Pyramids near the start of the main road to Upper Egypt, the Tariq Aswan. The Giseh district has a long and interesting history. The town of al-Giseh was officially founded in the fourth century BC at the place where the Nile crossed the established route between Heliopolis and Memphis. Memphis declined in importance with the growth of Christianity and became subordinate to Giseh, which was closer to the Babylon Fortress. 'Amr settled the Arab tribes of Himyar and Hamdan in the area after the Muslim conquest. In the following

the city a year or so before he married my mother and he ran a stall selling hot food. He had saved some money from the time he worked as a driver for the British during the war. When they had to leave, my parents went back to the village where my father was born, which is near Aswan in the very far south of the country. At that time they had just arranged my marriage to Ahmed, a man who lived in this part of the city, so I had to stay behind when my parents left. In the first few months I got to know Ahmed's maternal aunt and became close friends with his sisters. I still value their friendship and these women are like sisters despite all that's happened in the long years since then. When we were first married Ahmed was a good and respectful husband. Marriage itself was a frightening experience for a girl of just sixteen without a mother or sisters for support and reassurance. But my husband expected no more of me than is a wife's duty. I shared his bed and enjoyed keeping house, cooking his meals and washing and cleaning things for him. Ahmed for his part was determined to work hard and provide the money we needed. We had our separate duties and that's how things should be in a marriage.

My mother-in-law had sometimes been harsh to me before the wedding, but this isn't unusual because a woman has to be sure that her son is going to marry a girl with character and stamina. In my case it was particularly important since my parents were leaving the city and I

---

centuries Giseh remained a middle-sized town, but generally unimportant until in the nineteenth century Ismail Pasha, the francophile ruler, built a palace with gardens by Deschamps, now the Zoological Gardens. The ceremonial opening of the Suez Canal was accompanied by extensive rebuilding and redecoration. A new road to the Pyramids was constructed for the convenience of foreign visitors and guests of honour. When Egypt came under the British sphere of influence, considerable construction work was undertaken in Giseh and many grand villas were built along the Sh'al-Ahram (Pyramid Road). Since the mid 1940s there has been a boom in utility building in the Giseh area, especially in housing for engineers, teachers and other professionals.

would have no kin to turn to if the marriage went wrong. Of course nobody could have guessed how things would turn out in the end.

After a short while my mother-in-law seemed to think that I was turning out all right. She used to tease me by saying that I could feed a hungry crowd on a penny a day. She was only joking of course, but I was very thrifty and careful with money. In those days money seemed to go further than it does now. Now everyone has to struggle to make ends meet. Maybe this struggle appears worse for me because I'm alone and have to look after myself. But that's what happens to a woman who is cursed and childless. I often wonder what life would have been like if I'd been able to have just one son.

I was divorced about two years after my wedding day. I wasn't quite eighteen but I had failed to have children, the thing which is a women's greatest duty to her husband. I was only pregnant once in the two years I was married, but gave birth to a dead child. The dead baby was a girl and she came too early to have a chance of survival. My heart felt like it was breaking when I saw her because she was so tiny and very beautiful. I could see nothing to explain why she should have died, since she was so lovely. Her little nose and mouth were quite perfect and she looked so calm and peaceful. It seemed as if she hadn't been supposed to have a part in this world and was in Paradise already. Even now I often dream of my baby's face.

Anyway after the stillborn child I was never pregnant again and it was clear that I was infertile. I lost my husband because of this as I deserved to. A woman without children is like a well without water, she's quite useless! Indeed, maybe it's worse than that, after all someone might find a use for a deep dry hole.

My sisters-in-law remained good friends in those terrible days, even though you might consider that I had brought disgrace on their family by the divorce. They were

kind enough to ask a relative and neighbour to help me to
find rooms and a job. I couldn't stay in the family place
any longer, especially after Ahmed announced that he was
taking a new wife. May God forgive me, but at that time
I wanted this new wife of his to die. I have no grudge
against her now of course, but the grief, pain and shame
that I felt then made me hate her. Now I can only feel pity
for this woman, because over the years it's become public
knowledge that Ahmed isn't a very kind man or a good
husband. But when I was divorced everything seemed different because I wasn't very old and didn't have much
experience of life.

After the divorce it was agreed that I should keep the
clothing, furniture and utensils which I had brought to the
marriage. There weren't many things and they weren't
valuable, but I could have used these possessions to set up
home and begin a new life alone without having to start
from scratch. But Ahmed prevented me from collecting my
things and I had no one who was in a position to intervene
for me. My parents were too far away and naturally they
couldn't have come back to the city to assist a daughter
who had disgraced them.

I was lucky because Ahmed's sisters provided all kinds
of support. Although they couldn't help me to get my
things back, they gave me some of their own cooking pots
as tokens of friendship. Some years after this, about three
years later I think, Ahmed's paternal uncle came to my
rooms. He had a message from Ahmed's family that a cart
would be arriving with my possessions. My possessions
after all that time! By then they were practically useless,
quite worn out. They'd only been sent to me because Ahmed
had bought new things with the gifts of money he
got after the birth of his third son.

As I said before, Ahmed's wife has no easy life with him.
At times I'm relieved that I escaped her fate. Just after
Ahmed remarried and their first boy Mohammed was
born he went away to work in the oil industry. At that time

there was no shortage of work in the desert and men could earn a great deal of money there. This work and the big wages he earned gave Ahmed his foolish greedy notions. He came back here acting like he was a great lord. His family was well off then and I was happy for their good fortune, but of course this sort of luck always comes to a sudden end. When the money ran out it was clear what kind of a man he had become. Now he makes his wife take a job in the streets, a woman with six children! What kind of a life is that and what kind of a husband does that make him!

It can't be easy to be married to a man whose only love is money and material things. I have no interest in material things, that's not my problem. My terrible vice is childlessness, the curse of having no sons to protect me as I grow older and no daughters to make sure that I have enough to eat. Still I suppose I should be grateful that I am healthy enough to arrange my own life. I take in sewing work to keep food in my cupboard, but it's no disgrace to look after yourself in a world where there is neither father nor husband to provide for you. If Ahmed spent less money on foolish shows of wealth and on his fancy shoes and clothes, then his poor wife wouldn't have to suffer such shame by working in the streets from dawn to dusk!

Perhaps it's strange that all this talk has been about other people, about the man who divorced me, and his wife and children, but I feel like they are the only kin I have to discuss.

My sewing work keeps food in the cupboard and this keeps me alive. It's not so difficult for me as it is for other women without a husband. It's very hard to look after yourself when you're a widow or divorcee. Although I'm divorced myself, it is easier for me to work because I have no children. What really breaks my heart is to see young mothers working their fingers to the bone to provide for their little ones. If your husband can't earn enough for his family's needs then you're in a dreadful situation. It must be so painful to have beautiful children and not enough time to play with them.

I have to bear the burden of earning money because I'm childless and manless and I hope that I've found an honourable way of doing it. I can work at home and decide when and for how long I work each day. Abu Zeyad works for the factory owner and he brings the fabric and collects the finished items. I spend the morning tracing out the patterns and cutting the fabric and in the afternoon I stitch them together. These bits of fabric are the linings for bags or pouches. Some afternoons I can do housework or go to the market and sometimes I visit friends before finishing off the sewing late at night. If friends have problems with their work and children I like to help out if I can. It brings me great joy to look after their little ones for an afternoon, or anytime at all really. I don't think of it as a favour, it's much more of a privilege.

Naturally I'd much prefer not to work at all and be free from what they call a man's burden. I mean, women have many everyday chores to do at home, what with caring for their family, washing, brushing, cooking and so on, but that's what every woman plans for in life, it's a duty, it isn't a burden like men's work. There is little pleasure in working for money like men do, whereas women find pleasure in doing things for their husband and family.

My boss says my work is good and has asked me to take a job in the workshop, but I always refuse. The wages are higher if you work there but I prefer the privacy of working in my own home. Perhaps it is permissible for a young woman to do factory work to get money for her wedding. The important thing for the young women is that this work is temporary.* I'll have to continue working all my life.

---

* Most women who work before marriage take a job outside the home, which pays higher wages than home-based work. This enables them to contribute towards the costs of their wedding. The women and their kin always stress that this is only a temporary job until marriage, when their husbands will provide for them. What usually happens is that women start working again when they

Since this is the case I feel that I must do it in the most honourable way possible. I was brought up to think about work like my country relatives. I think that it's a bad thing if a woman of any age has to push her way through crowded streets like a man. Men belong in the streets, that's their proper place. Although my life has been blighted by having a body which refused to work like a woman's, I feel that it's important to behave like a good and proper woman in every other way I can.

If there had been any chance perhaps I would have married again. But no offer was made, it just didn't happen. People always know why divorces occur because it's impossible to hide something like that. Divorce is such a terrible thing. People here like to know about such terrible things and chew over the stories like sugar cane, they gnaw their way through the surface until they reach the satisfying core. No matter what the public version may be, people will get to the truth and they'll always know the full story, though they mightn't discuss it openly. In my own case there was never any secret about why Ahmed divorced me and so no other man would have been interested in marrying me.

If I'd moved to an area where I was unknown perhaps there would have been an opportunity to marry again. But it's likely that the man's enquiries eventually would have revealed the shame of my infertility. Listen to all these 'ifs' and 'maybes', it's a foolish old woman talking! To be quite honest I thank God that no second offer of marriage came. I know I would have been tempted to accept in order to avoid this lonely insecure life. But it's not right that a woman should get married out of fear of being alone, especially one who can't give her husband children. I'm also sure that the shame of being divorced a second time

---

have several children and their husbands' wages prove inadequate. At this time most women choose to work at home, because this enables them to look after domestic duties and not embarrass their husbands by being seen to work.

would have killed me, certainly a second divorce would
have been inevitable. I can imagine just what would have
followed that, the gossips would have been busy for weeks.
Harsh people would have said that death was a fitting end
for the woman who couldn't give birth!

I've heard that doctors can cure childless women,
although people say that it's dangerous and surely it's a sin
to tamper with what God has created? I don't have any
education and so I have no right to opinions about such
complicated things. But I can't silence the voice inside my
head which keeps asking why a woman's life should be
damned by her body's emptiness and uselessness? There
are so many things that I just can't work out however hard
I try. Of course God has intended things to be like this.
What troubles me is why I was given a brain which can
think and a heart which can feel inside the empty shell of
this faulty body.

So much has changed since I was a girl, when I had no
sad thoughts and worries. I remember that my girlfriends
and I always were afraid of acting without modesty or
being seen to behave in some shameful way that would
destroy our reputation. Most of the time we weren't sure
what a reputation was except that it meant the difference
between being married and being an old maid! There were
fewer girls to be seen in the streets then. Certainly very few
had a job and it was the same for married women too.

What has changed? We all hear what they say about
women being tainted by western ways, behaving like
whores, having no respect for family honour and so on. But
I feel that it might be the husbands who have changed
most. Poverty changes everyone. It forces women to earn
money and the husbands to cripple themselves with a
desire to be wealthy. If this is true, then it's not that women
are neglecting old values but that men are creating new
ones.

One of the greatest problems is that a person's real value
comes from their money in the modern world. Girls risk

their honour to earn a lot of money outside the home with just a scarf to protect them! Some even are foolish enough to think that men find their wages more attractive than a good heart. Maybe some men do, but in any case that's all part of what's wrong with the modern world. When I was a girl I cared more about the things inside my head than whatever was wrapped around it. This new fashion for veils seems to be a way of proclaiming: 'Look at me! Look at my beautiful veil!' At times I think attention to veiling is just an attempt to appear modest so that people can work and try to get rich. I'm sure that it comes from people's greed and love of money.

People use money as a short cut to get whatever they want. Still, people are poor and being poor makes you want immediate satisfaction, even in things that might destroy you in the end. You can see this in Ahmed's marriage. His wife may have a television but she isn't happy. How can she be content when she has so little time to spend with her beautiful children. How I envy her those lovely children, more than money or even marriage.

Marriage and money are like spinning tops which brush each other then spin off in opposite directions. A wife chases after them in vain. She tries to keep them both going but it's impossible unless she cuts herself in two. Perhaps the problem is that the tops are spinning too fast and destroying things between husbands and wives. It's like we're living in a sandstorm of confusion and families have lost sight of their duty to each other. I think that men are too weak to see this clearly. I mean they only seem to think about money when they look for a wife. They marry a girl who can buy her own wedding gifts and only think about the money they're saving. It doesn't occur to them to consider the responsibility of providing for a wife and children.

What would I want from life if things had been different? One thing for sure is a good husband. If I was young again and if I wasn't cursed with an empty womb and could know the joys of motherhood, I'd rather marry a poor man and have his children than live like a slave to some factory job in a house like a palace! Are children loved and cared for because they are surrounded by luxuries? Do television sets make good mothers?

I know that I shouldn't talk like this or dream about impossible things. Families and husbands are not for me. You know why these things have no part in the story of my life. I adore my friends' children and delight in their company. This is enough for me and I'm grateful for it. Maybe there are things that I have forgotten, and perhaps I've not told my story properly or clearly, but when I started to think about my life this is what I most wanted to say.

Amira was sitting in her usual place rocking Oum Sherif's baby when the following tale was told.

THE WORTH OF A POT

This is a tale of sorrow and despair, but one also tinged with mysteries which might lighten the spirits and tease a smile from tear-stained faces. There is a woman, a man and a spirit child. But they are not the main characters, because this is the tale of a cooking pot. The tale begins and ends with this pot, and the same pot turns up at every stage in between.

There was a middle-sized pot which formed part of a young bride's dowry. It was just an ordinary pot, not particularly shiny or attractive or interesting, nor was it the largest pot she had. It wasn't big enough for a family stew and it was too big to boil an egg in. Let's say that at most it was a pot for rice for two. The sad thing is that this was an empty pot for a very long time. The young bride woke early every morning with a head full of delicious plans. She would reach for her enormous stew pot and pack it full of

the tightest wrapped vine-leaf parcels you could imagine.*
Each stuffed vine leaf glistened greeny-black and hidden
inside the parcel was a moist core of tender meat, moist
rice and exciting spices. She would sing half-remembered
songs from her mother's village as she poured stock into
the pot, covering her beautiful leaves with this golden
liquid. With the meal prepared well in advance of her
husband's hunger, the young bride could set about the less
satisfying tasks of the day, and because she was a young
bride she still took uncalled-for pleasure in every chore.
The dust on the floor and the muck on her man's shirt were
a delight to her. She had a lot to prove to him and feared
that some evening a frown would crease his brow when he
spotted a speck of grit lurking under the table. The broom
and the wash tub and the big cooking pot were the tools
of her trade and they made up her entire world.

The middle-sized pot hung over the stove and waited
like a virgin. It was still unused, being too small for the vine
leaves. She hadn't discovered any particular use for it. An
empty pot is an ugly thing in any woman's life and should
be kept well out of sight. This thought occurred to the bride
one day and so she took it down from its hook. The bride
put the pot in a trunk under the bed lest its apparent
uselessness provoke some criticism from her husband or
in-laws. The neglected little pot lay there and gathered
dust in the darkness, waiting and listening.

As time passed there were great changes in that house-

---

* Wara Einab, or stuffed vine leaves, is a popular dish throughout the Middle
East and in most Mediterranean countries. The recipe has many variations,
but as a general rule rice and minced lamb or beef are used in the hot version
of the dish described in the tale. The leaf is spread flat, vein side up and a
teaspoon of filling is placed in the centre near the stem edge. The stem is folded
over the filling, both sides of the leaf are then folded towards the centre and
the leaf is rolled like a small cigar. Stuffing the leaves is a delicate operation
and the end result must be firm but not over-firm if the 'parcel' is to remain
intact during cooking.

hold. The bride, now not so young and not so innocent, was heard weeping and harsh things were said. The little pot listened in horror and understood. It would not forget these things and could not repeat them for it had no voice. The empty pot lay forgotten in the trunk under the bed. When the master of the house sent his wife away and divorced her the pot in the trunk was left behind. The cause of all the tears and curses was so unmentionable that the bride did not dare to try to get her things back.* The woman had just disappeared as far as the pot was concerned. Even the big pots that had been so proud and full of good things were abandoned in the flight and fell into the hands of the new woman in the kitchen.

Something else had witnessed all the changes. There was a magical spirit which clung to the hem of the bride's dress. Not that the woman knew, of course. It was quite invisible to everyone. This spirit was always there, though nobody would ever suspect that a wonderful thing would be attracted by such a woman. Where did it come from? What did it want? Who can say and who would dare to! But the important thing is that although the woman often wept and cried out that her life was empty, she was not alone in her empty rooms.

* Islamic law stipulates that divorced women should receive financial compensation and maintenance payments. However, divorce among the poor tends to diverge from the law. In practice few divorcees from poor families receive maintenance payments from their ex-husbands. Where property of any kind is a valuable asset and difficult to replace, a divorced woman will go to a great deal of trouble to maintain possession of the household goods and gifts which she was given (or bought) during the marriage. Women commonly provide for their economic security after divorce in two additional ways. The first is to amass gifts of jewellery, usually gold, which are considered to be the sole property of the wife. The second is an optional but more formal agreement that a fixed sum of money will be paid to the wife if the marriage ends in divorce. This involves the couple's parents designating a portion of the obligatory wedding gift (from husband to wife) as compensation for death or divorce. Most parents broach this sensitive subject during marriage negotiations in order to give their daughter some economic security against divorce although, understandably, people feel that it must be handled carefully so as not to create distrust and bad feeling.

Meantime old people still groaned on towards death and children still howled their way into the world. During those years the woman grew older and more accustomed to her solitary life, while the spirit floated around behind her. Now the pain of her secret shame and her physical loneliness took on a different shape. At first the pain inside had been like boiling oil, then it began to congeal. In time it set rock hard and made her insides like concrete. It was a heavy weight to carry around but it was also an inner shield against further wounds. There were tongues stabbing her like daggers every day, bitter dreams throbbing in her head at night, and news about the world she had lost flying from all directions like poisoned arrows. But none of these cruel things could pierce the woman's hard ravaged core and bleed her dry.

It was that time of night when the sun's heat starts to creep out of a corrugated iron roof and tries to suffocate half-sleeping humans. The woman's spirit flitted free over the bed roll and looked down on her chosen charge. She, because this was a female spirit, could hear sad little noises coming from the woman's mouth: soft moans like the cry from a kitten or a baby. This was a beautiful spirit indeed. If you could see her you would be enchanted by her sweet smile and delicate features and graceful movements. The spirit floated down and nestled against the dreaming women's breasts and stroked the woman's hair. There was magic at work and all the forces at the beautiful spirit's command filled the room. In the flutter of a drowsy eyelid the woman was no longer alone. Her mattress became a trampoline filled with mischievous jinn and the gambolling plump spirits of unborn children. They giggled and jumped around the room. They bounced from the mattress to the light bulb to the ceiling and back again. In the shadowy corner of the room a large rat stopped scratching in the dirt, momentarily transfixed by the spectacle. The rat scuttled off when a fat jinn dived towards it with bared fangs. The room took on a silvery glow from all the energy

these creatures generated. The spirit had transformed
the empty room into a carnival. The spirit watched as the
creatures she had summoned grew tired of bounding
around in the heat. One by one they floated down to the
mattress-edge, paused there like naughty toddlers anxious
to avoid a scolding, then they pursed their lips and with a
sudden kiss they all disappeared back inside the woman's
head. Finally the spirit curled up beside the woman under
the covers and heard something like a chuckle escape from
her sleeping lips.

The next day when the sun was high over the city there
were interesting events taking place behind a certain door.
Clouds of dust were puffing out of the window of one house
in the neighbourhood, accompanied by grunts and muffled
curses. Brooms were forced into unaccustomed corners
and grimy hands rattled the long-forgotten contents of a
bride's old battered trunk. The trunk was pulled out of its
resting place under the bed. It was coated with muck which
stuck to the surface like a second skin. The bed itself was
in not much better shape. The covers were stained with
unmentionable things, shit being one of the more men-
tionable substances. But dirt is not always disgusting and
the old trunk was shrouded in nothing worse than the products of time and neglect. The pot inside the trunk had just
been shaken to life. The old virgin pot was as empty as it
always had been. A few tatty bits of cotton cloth and some
mis-matched dishes had been its companions in the trunk
since that long-ago wedding.

These were the odd things nobody wanted because at
that time nobody could find a use for them. A man was
cursing the dust and the mess in the room in a rough
familiar voice. The pot had heard these nasty curses
before. It recalled the old arguments and the cause of the
divorce. But the pot also remembered the power of fate and
it waited. There were other voices in the room: a veritable
wailing of children wanting food, a hopeless mother's
demands and meaningless pleas to the hungry brood, and

the man's angry threats again, which now rose to a crescendo of fury and drowned the noise made by everyone else. At this point a skilled listener, such as the pot, would have detected the clatter of distant hooves as a donkey cart drew nearer and then stopped outside the house. There was the sound of a visitor entering. A very skilled listener would have guessed the meaning behind the tell-tale stutter of curses which brought the man to a sudden silence. It was the kind of silence which suggested that the world had come to an end. Without further warning the trunk was swung up from the floor, thrust into strong arms, bundled on to the cart and ferried through bumpy streets.

Where was it being taken? Another wedding perhaps? The trunk was a bride's trunk, a small but hardy casket usually stuffed with a girl's trousseau. What was inside? This kind of trunk is usually full of a bride's best china and tableware, her very best embroidered cloths and precious knick-knacks. The occasion? Usually a happy one. Never mind that a bride's trunk hints at the insecurity of marriage: the black shadow of divorce which hangs over every bride. A bride counts all the treasures in her trunk and values them like old friends. After all, they are the only thing any bride can be sure of in her future life. They are her last source of security if all else fails. But of course this is an old bride's trunk and there are no wedding celebrations and no treasures inside it. Remember that the wedding was over long ago, the bride was abandoned and her treasures had been stolen by another wife. What then of the trunk? Is this just a journey to the dump?

Earlier that day the woman had taken a little longer with her morning housework. She was trying to shake off the memory of a curious dream and this made every task seem more complicated than usual. The dust seemed glued to her rugs and the water only trickled from the pump however much effort she put into the work. She laid out a few vine leaves and salted the mixture in the bowl, looking forward to filling each leaf and carefully folding the plump bundles. This was a favourite meal but one that she did not often prepare. It was a lot of time and bother for a meal for one. Today the woman welcomed the chance to concentrate on a task which demanded precision and each little bundle was a work of art by the time she had finished. She remembered when she used to stuff enough leaves for a feast. Now she prepared just a few, there were barely enough leaves to cover the base of a small pot, but they were expertly made. The vine leaves glistened with the same beautiful greeny-black colour as other leaves in another kitchen a long time before. She was watching the stock bubble when the trunk arrived.

The woman was struck dumb with surprise and paralysed with horror. The man who delivered the trunk was embarrassed. He behaved with great respect, obviously sorry for her. He could see that she was not prepared for this unexpected gift. The woman managed to thank him for his trouble, because it was a kind of a gift, even if it was one poisoned by the past and quite worthless. The man departed as suddenly as he had arrived and left the woman alone with the trunk. She stared at the trunk from afar as if afraid to touch it. The concrete which had hardened inside her threatened to break and release a new flood of pain. She thought that this time she might die of reopened wounds. The trunk lay on the rug by the stove. It was quite out of place in the spotless room and the crust of muck on the lid seemed an outrage. The woman felt depressed by the sight of this dirt in her neat and tidy home. She was angry and confused, as if the trunk had insulted her by arriving unannounced and unwanted. The trunk was an undesirable guest from the past. She grew more angry and struggled with the memories and emotions associated with the trunk. It was too bad. There was was just one thing she could do.

She took the trunk outside and scrubbed it with soap and water until every speck of dust and grime was gone. The old leather surface was scarred and cracked, and the catch was broken. It wasn't much of a trunk but she might use it for something. Inside, away from the curious eyes which watched from surrounding doorsteps, she opened the lid and wept. There she found the rags, the broken dishes and the pot. This is my fate, she thought. This is a fit trousseau for the future. No fine fabrics, no pretty tablecloths, no valuable ornaments. The woman remembered the impressive collection of goods which had made up her original trousseau. Now there were no treasures in her trunk; gone were the shining copper trays, the crisp linen and silken embroidery threads, the delicate glass bowl and precious silver dish. The remnant mocked her. She thought that the ugly things in the trunk were the kind of trousseau she deserved. Her tears fell like rain in the lonely room, the only sound was a steady dripping as they splashed on the trunk lid. The woman wept for a long time. The woman's guardian spirit was dismayed. Such spirits have little interest in what happens in our world and no knowledge about men's petty plans and practices. The return of the trunk had not been foreseen or expected. Remember that spirits only affect our secret life and they only have our emotions to work with. The spirit peered into the trunk and looked at the wreck of the trousseau, knowing that she could do little to change what had passed, she could only watch and wait for the night. The beautiful spirit was full of compassion for the woman because of a secret sorrow which bound them together, she was linked to the woman by a tragedy which this tale can't reveal.

At last the woman wiped away her tears, as if the unseen presence had been of some comfort. She got to her feet and the spirit followed her to the stove where the vine leaves were still simmering in the stock. The meal was ready and the moon would soon be rising to bring an end to this curious day. The woman cleared a place on the table and set out a plate, knife, spoon and glass with the mechanical routine of the lonely diner. She spooned out the vine leaves and rice and left the meal to cool. There was half a bucket of water left over from the morning chores and the woman poured all of it into the washing-up bowl. The cooking utensils were always scrubbed before she ate. But there was one extra job to be tackled before dinner tonight. This woman, with the determination of ten men and the courage of one hundred, had vowed not to weep again. She would put her past behind her.

She went over to the open trunk and examined each object in turn. The tattered lengths of cotton were too poor even for her. She lifted the broken pieces of crockery and set them on top of the bits of cloth. A brief critical look settled their fate. She grasped the corners of the fabric and made a bundle of the old dishes, a firm package of the past, as neat as her stuffed vine leaves. She set them aside as rubbish and took some satisfaction from the thought that this would make an intriguing addition to the dump for malicious observers. Then the woman's attention returned to the pot. It was not a particularly impressive pot, not very big, not conveniently small and certainly not shiny. But neither was it worthless. It had a certain practical value as well as a comforting familiarity. She would scrub it until it was as good as new. She would be sure to find some use for it and fill it after all.

The women were all quiet and watchful when the tale finished. There was nothing like the loud exclamations of praise for a tale which I had come to expect. Everyone was moved by the tale and there were tears in most women's eyes. Gradually more typical high spirits returned and the storyteller's skill was the main topic of discussion. As the women departed, the hostess, Oum Mohammed, had to clear away the tea things alone for the first time. Amira had gone. We had all glanced at Amira occasionally while the tale was unfolding and she had appeared to be listening with her usual intent but impassive expression. She must have slipped away without a word just after the tale ended but no one had noticed. Fatima, the baby Amira had been holding, was asleep in her blanket in the corner of the room.

OUM IDRIS: A DETERMINED WOMAN

Within minutes of her arrival Oum Idris is in the centre of things since she is a dependable source of the most up-to-date, detailed versions of local news. She always sits as close to the middle of the room as possible, which suits her role of chief commentator and leader of audience participation during a tale. Oum Idris always can be relied upon to give a constant running commentary to any tale, no matter how long or highly charged with emotion. She is the most vocal and enthusiastic member of the audience when a tale is underway and is never stuck for a sharp, well timed comment. Her witty remarks and interjections are the cause of much amusement and they often remain in circulation long after they first were heard. Oum Idris has been known to tell good tales herself, although she has never done so within the story telling circle. In private she once said that the best storytelling depends on being sensitive to people's feelings, and admitted that this is not one of her foremost qualities. Oum Idris' daring tongue makes her a popular character at the gatherings, but essentially she remains outside the pale of polite company. The explanation for this can be found in Oum Idris' life story, which she told in the following words.

My earliest memory is of a journey, long dusty trails and long days and nights when my parents and I walked from our village to the city. I was a young girl then. Now that I'm growing old I have a lifetime's experience to reflect on. I have known both good and bad sides of life and have been through quite a few things which make me special — not that everybody would agree that special is the most appropriate word! I have one son and he's not exactly the son every woman would desire, but Idris is on the right path now and I think he will prove his worth in the end. *

---

* Idris was one of the neighbourhood's most undesirable characters. He had a history of petty criminal activities, from theft to handling stolen goods. He was mixed up with men reputed to be drug dealers, which attracted the attention of the police. This was the final straw for his mother, who put all her

I have three daughters as well, all married now and off my hands, anyway unlike my son, they were such good girls that I hardly noticed them. That's how a lot of things are in this world, trouble sticks in people's minds.

The journey I mentioned was not really the best place to start my story, but it's the one I chose for reasons that will become clear as I go on.

My parents were good people. My father was a small farmer who eventually lost his fight with poor soil and turned towards the city. That decision was the one which changed the whole course of my life. Who knows how different things would have been for me if I had grown up a village girl. When I look back there isn't much that I can remember about our early days in the city. I was old enough to be married and my parents were desperate to find me a husband, even though they had little money. Of course the fact that they were almost penniless meant that once they succeeded in finding me a husband, they would have one less mouth to feed! Things are as simple as that sometimes. But in my case things are rarely simple!

If I say something about one of the main events in the story of my life it will explain that last comment. I was very ill as a child and it was so serious that I almost died. Naturally I don't recall that period well. There are lots of things which people told me about afterwards which I only half-remember, and now all these years later most of it seems like a dream. But I can recall the anxious faces peering at me in the midst of my fever and I'll never forget the range of cures which were tried out on me. I got better in the end, but I wasn't cured. Oh no, the cure came a long

---

energies into finding him a wife, convinced that the responsibilities of marriage would force him to change his ways. It took all of his mother's considerable skill as a matchmaker to find a wife for Idris, and Oum Idris made several unsuccessful attempts before a marriage was arranged. Oum Idris was triumphant when her plan finally worked and Idris appeared to be a reformed character after several months of married life, a fact which was reflected in local gossip.

time later, in the city itself. By then I was well enough to play like ordinary children and to torment the goats I was supposed to look after and, finally, to make the journey to the city with my parents. As I said before, that journey to the city is the best place to begin my life story. My illness and the journey to the city are the two things that I'll mention most.

There is a lot of talk these days about infections and germs and things like this, so you might understand my illness in those terms. I had a kind of internal disease for a big part of my adult life, not one that could be cured in the normal way. When I fell ill as a child, the village healers were useless, and I'm sure that scientific doctors and experts in hospitals would have been just as powerless. My disease was one which attacked the mind, not that you'd know it now since I must be one of the most determined and strong-willed women around. What I'm talking about in this round-about way has to do with the spirit world. Country people recognise the danger and the importance of all the spirits you can't see, and they respect them too. On the other hand, life in the city influences people and changes them. It encourages people to forget about country ways and makes some grow sceptical and ignore spiritual and supernatural things. In areas like this you have both the sceptics and those with first-hand knowledge of the spirits' influence on people.

My own trouble had to do with a certain spirit which chose to interfere in my life. It took hold of me during the illness I mentioned, at least that was the first sign of its presence and some healers tried to deal with it then. But they failed, worse luck! Meantime I came to Cairo, became a woman, then a wife, then a mother, and all the time the spirit was still there making me think bad things and behave in quite awful, unacceptable ways. I wasn't a good mother until the time of my cure, which shows just how powerful and dangerous these spirits can be. Imagine, they can even warp a woman's strongest natural instincts!

The story of my life jumps from event to event in this rather haphazard way because it is difficult for me to distinguish clear links between my youth and my adult life. Unlike most other people, my early memories are altered by the fact that the spirit controlled me, and this determines my view of myself at that time. I did not escape from the chains of that spirit until I was twenty-five years old. Before that I had no freedom from the spirit's evil influence. That is the absolute truth of the matter, my childhood was stolen and it was the same with my years as a young wife and mother, until I woke up, or was reborn you might say, at the age of twenty-five!

I had four children, first the girls, then Idris. They were all born before my cure, although still youngsters when I was finally freed from the spirit. I will always thank God that they were not fully grown when my senses were restored and so I had some chance to make up for my past neglect of them. I would rather forget those years, twenty years of my life were lost in a bad dream and I hope that they stay missing, since it's just too awful to think about them. It would kill me to recall exactly how the spirit affected my behaviour. Maybe God will give me an extra-long life to make amends. Just think, if I die when I'm sixty, in real terms I'd only be about forty years old, the age I am right now! I can begin my story properly now because everything I've said so far is a kind of background to what has happened during my life.

My husband Sherif died last year, God rest his soul, and he was a good man and he made a good husband. My parents chose an excellent husband for me. They must have judged that his calm manner and mild temper would make him likely to stand by me, however mad the spirit caused me to be. My parents did not live long enough to see me cured, but they knew Sherif would do his duty and not abandon the woman he had married. They must also have known that he would do his best to find a solution to the problems my spirit caused. When the spirit demanded

expensive things Sherif always bought them; when I went
mad and smashed dishes he did not try to stop me in order
to save the pottery, and when I was in a complete fury he
beat me until the spirit was quiet. He always did the right
thing, although he didn't know about the problem when
he married me.

I was very attractive as a girl and that was lucky because
young men have very little sense when it comes to looking
for a wife. Of course that's why wise old parents make
the final choice. Still, my looks meant that it was not too
difficult for my parents to omit mention of my illness when
they were arranging the marriage. There are those who
would say that this was dishonest, but what alternative was
there? How could they admit that their beautiful daughter,
one of the best catches from a new family in the neighbourhood, was possessed by a spirit of greed and avarice?
A revered pious family might take this approach, but such
people can usually afford to feed themselves, my parents
couldn't!

Sherif, my husband, did not have a very normal
domestic life with me until the day of my cure. He said that
the greatest day of his life was when the Sheikha, the wise
woman who drove the spirit out, declared: 'Look! This is
your wife. Praise God and take her home in peace.' I
remember that he said that the sight of me feeding Idris the
following morning made his heart glow with joy. It's not
easy to explain, but I don't remember feeling an immediate change after the cure, and I don't think I was aware
that I was behaving in a different way after the spirit
was driven out. You see, I didn't know that I was being
possessed by a spirit when it was inside me. I thought that
I was normal and I wasn't aware that I behaved very badly
at its command. After my cure, when I really was normal,
I was unaware of that too. It's only in recent years when
I look back at my life and look at other people around me
that I understand the difference between badness and evil.
The first comes from bad people who have gone wrong

because of a loss of self-control, but the second comes from the spirits and is beyond human control.

My daughters grew up into pretty young women and now they have children of their own. My daughters have sweet tempers and are polite and obedient to everyone, and my grandchildren are a delight and just as sweet as their mothers. Naturally my daughters' husbands are good men, I saw to that. Sherif took charge of the wedding plans but I made sure that we would only consider the best candidates possible. I wanted my daughters to have strong, quiet and reliable husbands. This is not the type of man which makes your heart shiver and burn at the same time, but the least exciting men are the safest choice. They make the best husbands. I know!

My skill in matchmaking is well known and I don't mind boasting about it a bit. Finding a good combination of families and individuals requires a special art and a lot of imagination. You have to think ahead and speculate on how this girl and boy will turn out in the years to come. You have to look at the couple's kin and try to spot certain qualities which are as yet hidden in the young people. Good matchmaking ensures a good marriage, in so far as you can ever be sure of anything!

You couldn't find a much better example of this than in the marriage of my son Idris and Mona, his new wife. They were made for each other because life has battered them both a little. This type of equality and balance is the important thing.* It isn't up to us to judge people and to proclaim them either all good or all bad. All we can do is look for good things and avoid the bad if we can't understand it. A skilful matchmaker works to find a pair who will bring a reasonable mixture of human qualities to a mar-

---

* Equality between husband and wife is considered to be an essential factor in a good marriage. Particular attention is given to a prospective spouse's family background, reputation and prestige and income and education levels.

riage. Opposites might attract but that's a terrible basis for a match between a man and woman.

Idris has not been an easy son and his problems are really a reflection of mine. Idris was the youngest of my children and I think that he was more deeply disturbed than the others, first by my illness and then by my cure. He suffered most neglect when I was in the final and the worst phase of my madness. I will never forgive myself for this as long as I live, although of course I wasn't actually responsible for my illness. After I was free of the spirit, suddenly I was a model mother. I devoted myself to my husband and children, particularly to Idris. This was a big mistake. Every time he fell over I showered him with too many kisses and comforting words. I played with him for hours when other boys were playing with their friends in the street. I tried to satisfy his every whim to try to make up for the kind of mother I was before. It's possible that I lavished too much attention on him. A sudden change in a mother's behaviour confuses and upsets a young child. Of course I also have to admit that I can't be blamed for all the things that went wrong later when he was no longer a scared little boy.

Like everyone else, Idris certainly has a lot of black marks on his character which he put there himself. In the past he did a lot of bad things when he got involved with some disreputable characters from outside the neighbourhood. This made things even worse. People in this area stick together, they don't look elsewhere for help or expect any to come from outside. Outsiders are bad news and of course they have a worse reputation.* People here rely on each other, so it's really bad if someone turns

---

* Popular stereotypes of city dwellers (from other neighbourhoods of course) illustrate the evils which follow when people are influenced by modernity and urban life. In particular, local people warn against the fat cats (al Kotat el Soman) who have acquired wealth by dubious means and thrive by exploiting poor and credulous migrants.

away from his own people and then falls in with criminals from other areas. Idris was associated with these outsiders and because of this he disgraced the community as well as himself and his family. But all that is past history, although there was a time in my life when I never thought that I would dare to say that. Still, I believe that nothing in the human world is all bad and that all worthwhile things have a happy conclusion. Idris and his wife are a perfect example of the truth of this.

Mona is a fine young woman, I'm growing very fond of her. She is strong and sensible and from a good family. But she has had more than her share of trouble in the past and gossips spent a lot of time and energy trying to blacken her name. The difficult time Mona experienced before Idris married her has taught her some valuable lessons about life.* Now she has seized this chance of a new beginning, which makes me very proud of her. She tries to prove her worth in every act on a daily basis, and that is how I try to live. Perhaps this explains why we are becoming friends, an unlikely thing between a man's mother and his young wife. Our feelings towards each other are not very typical

---

* The shadow over Mona's past reputation concerns a broken engagement after her former fiance's public accusation of sexual indiscretion with another man. Mona lived in a neighbouring district of the city, although news of this disgrace reached the neighbourhood where Oum Idris lives. This convinced Oum Idris that Mona's family might consider a proposal of marriage to her equally disgraced son. Mona's parents were keen to get their daughter married as soon as possible in order to salvage what remained of their good family name. The man who had broken the engagement had not reclaimed the engagement gifts he had given Mona so Idris 'inherited' them and was spared the expense of buying new gifts. The wedding was arranged quickly and Mona was glad of the chance to escape from her home district. As soon as his impending marriage was announced Idris went to great lengths to insist that the accusations of a sexual liaison against Mona were false. He also initiated a rumour that Mona's previous fiance had broken the engagement because he had lost the money for the wedding feast in a card game. This story seemed to be accepted once the 'true characters' of Mona and Idris emerged after their marriage. There was no further mention of the couple's troubled past and local gossips became preoccupied with the extent of the changes in the former deviants' behaviour.

of a mother-in-law and daughter-in-law. This is because we have much more in common than just a bond to a certain man. Mona and I both know what it's like to have to start life again and forget about the past. That marriage between my son and Mona gave both of them an opportunity to turn over a new leaf and forget about the past.

A new start to life is a precious gift. The mysterious paths our lives take only make sense to God, all we can hope for is the chance to try to undo the bad we have done. I also believe that it doesn't matter whether our sins were deliberate or accidental.

I think about things like this when I remember the journey from my parents' village to the city. The memory of the hardship my parents and I suffered on our journey has always stayed with me, even during the worst of my madness.

This makes me think that the journey itself marked the beginning of a new life, my second life, although of course I wasn't fully cured until the Sheikha recognised my affliction and cast out the spirit. The experience of that difficult journey may have been a way of earning the chance to be free from the spirit's evil influence. I believe that we all struggle every day in the hope of such chances.

One evening Oum Idris was being particularly candid and cutting. Everyone was amused by her description of a well known pious neighbour's complete change of heart about Idris and his new wife. Oum Idris had told this woman that she was first on her son's list of prospective co-wives. Later that evening the following tale was told.

THE MOST PRECIOUS POSSESSIONS

This is a tale of possession and liberation, of evil and innocence, of a struggle against wickedness and a struggle for good. The strands are tightly interwoven. Individual threads are almost indistinguishable in all the best weaving,

but not quite. This is a tale which will separate the one
thread from the other.

A travelling musician came east from the desert towards
the city. He had played in every village of any worth
throughout the land. He was weary after a long journey,
but not just tired in body. His spirit was troubled by a
dream which pursued him along the dirt tracks and paved
roads out of a certain village. The dream visited him every
night and the memory of the dream haunted him by day.
The musician tried to interpret the dream and find an
explanation for it. But now, being so familiar with its
images, he had to admit that the dream must be a sign of
his own madness. The musician could make no sense of it.

A little girl sat by a canal and carelessly tossed pebbles
into the foul-smelling water. It was dusk and there was a
smell of danger in the air. A man was watching her. He
was thinking that she shouldn't be there on the edge of the
village, all alone, away from her mother and father. The
little girl started to laugh but it was not a pleasant sound.
The pebbles were still splashing into the water, but more
violently now, as if the child was tormenting some invisible
monster on the river bed. The laughter grew louder and
raucous like the cackle of an old crone. It was a knowing
sort of laughter which spoke of delight in wickedness, of
forbidden pleasures and sins of every unspeakable kind.
It could not be the little girl's laughter, it was not possible
that this sound could come from an innocent child. The
man was fearful but did not know why.

He started to move towards the little girl, she was in
terrible danger. He wanted to save her, but he did not
know the source of the evil which threatened her. He
was close by, but his feet were as heavy as lead and he
could hardly move. The weeds were wrapping themselves
around his ankles, binding him to their stems, joining him
to their roots. He fought against them with a fury born
of terror. He was almost behind her now, almost close
enough to reach out and pull her away from the canal. The

wicked laughter went on and on, now punctuated with little squeals and cries and groans. The water was rippling and bubbling but not from the child's stones. The man's fingers brushed the fringe of her shawl as he tried to get a firm grip on it. The sound of the splashing water and the wicked laughter grew louder and more disturbing. Suddenly the water erupted in a fountain of evil-smelling slime, something was coming up from the depths of the canal, throwing up a deep wave. The man cried: 'God of mercy help her, save her! Help me, save me!' Soaked through with sweat and shaking with horror, the musician always woke with those pleas ringing in his ears.

A poor family struggled up the last hill on their hope-filled journey to the city. All their meagre possessions were strapped to one small donkey. They had come a long way from a country with stony soil and dried-up irrigation channels. They had abandoned the land of their ancestors just as its bounty had abandoned them. The head of the family led the party of three: his wife, his daughter and his scrawny beast of burden. The girl chattered excitedly. She was glad to have left the enclosed world of the village behind her. She was full of dreams about city life and what it would offer her. The promise of adventures, challenges, rewards and riches lay at the very core of her excitement. The girl had been thinking the same thought throughout the long journey: 'Everything will be new and all of it will be grand and special and splendid!' The mother plodded along beside the girl. The girl was just sixteen and her mother barely twice that age, but side by side the older woman looked like the girl's old grandmother because she was worn down with obvious concerns and secret fears. The mother was sullen and silent. She suddenly frowned at the daughter as if she could read her mind and was rebuking the girl for her optimism.

The demon couldn't believe its luck. It was also excited by the prospect of city life and full of wicked schemes. It stretched out its long claws in anticipation of the arrival.

It was one of the lesser evil spirits but, despite that, not any less wicked or capable of turning a life on to the dark path. It had discovered a perfect tool for future use and had taken possession of it back in a certain village. The demon lay dormant, enjoying the waves of anxiety, fear and bad feeling which flowed from mother to daughter. In the meantime it was content to wait for its chance to take full control of the girl when she was enticed by wicked city ways.

The family settled into the routine of a new life in the crowded city. Local people got to know them and helped out in a hundred small ways like the poor always do, conscious that they are all caught in the same hopeless trap. The husband and wife struggled to set up a home for their daughter, knowing that the sooner they established a reputation and some funds, the better the girl's marriage prospects. The girl slipped into city life as if she had been born to it. The parents worried at the ease of their daughter's transformation.

The girl's excited chattering now concerned down-town fashions, western magazines, American movies and the wonders of lip gloss and false eyelashes. It seemed that the hum and buzz of the city had driven out all memory of her good rural upbringing. The demon relished every outward appearance of its influence on the girl. It slowly worked its way to the surface through each of her new interests in luxury and with each new love of extravagance. The demon's presence within was apparent in the envious gleam of her eyes when she gazed at television images of excess wealth.

By this time she was no longer a girl on the edge of womanhood, but a desirable woman. Her abundant flesh had a rich glow, fuelled by the demon within. The woman was in the demon's grip and she grew more and more fond of luxury. She made constant demands on her parents for expensive things, each one more impossible than the last. The weary couple were at their wits' end, their only child seemed to want to bleed them dry of what small savings they had built up through austerity. A wedding was the obvious solution to their problems. The mother flushed out a decent husband from the swarm of men who had been feasting their eyes on her desirable daughter.

The bride was disappointed with her parents' choice, but gave no sign of it, knowing that any husband is better than none. He was far from the type of husband she had desired, being neither dashing nor filthy rich. It wasn't that he was a cruel or unjust husband, quite the contrary in fact, but, horror of horrors, he was ordinary! He was just an ordinary poor man from a poor area with some small ambitions and still smaller dreams. True to tell, there is nothing very interesting to say about the husband, which is just as well because this is not his tale. Children came to bless the marriage, but the demon barely noticed them, much like the woman herself. Caught up in the wicked weave of the demon's demands, the woman spent each day in a haze of envy and covetousness which clouded her awareness of everything else.

It was the time of Great Feast* and local people had been preparing for the celebration for days in advance. However, the woman's only thoughts were on the new dress she would wear. It was a splendid dress, rich in fabric and richer in colours, a rainbow of a garment. It fitted like a glove and showed off her fine figure. It fell around her ankles in luxurious folds which swished and flapped with the slightest movement, a sure sign of costly fabric. Her husband had taken longer than usual to get the dress for her because it had been very expensive. She had been impatient with him, though careful not to make him angry with too many reminders. In a rare moment when she

* The Great Feast or the Sacrificial Feast (Id al Kabir or Id al Adha) is celebrated throughout the Muslim world to mark the sacrifice of sheep during the Hajj (pilgrimage to Mecca). This is one of the greatest religious festivals. The Feast is celebrated on the tenth of the month of al Hajj in memory of the prophet Ibrahim. People buy new clothes for the occasion, give each other presents and celebrate the holiday with specially prepared dishes.

was not obsessed with the latest object of her desire, she wondered if it was strange that he never refused her greedy requests. Strange too that the neighbours hardly noticed her lovely new things and never admired them until she forced a reluctant word or two from their thin lips. But such thoughts never lasted for long. The demon recovered its hold on the woman and flooded her with a new stream of madness and envy.

The people of the area were rushing about in excitement on the morning of the feast day. The air was full of a hundred smells of good things to eat, all lovingly prepared for the celebration. A travelling musician rested against the wall of the mosque and watched the crowds gather in the square, softly strumming the strings of his instrument.* The musician bowed in respect to an old woman who made slow progress through the throng and stopped not far from him. The old woman and the musician exchanged customary greetings and fell into a polite silence, aware of each other but maintaining the proper distance between strangers. The curious thing is that, although strangers, their lives were to intertwine that very same day.

Now the musician began to play in earnest. He swept his bow across the instrument to the delight of the crowd and produced a cycle of tunes. Assorted children capered about in imitation of the skilful dances of their older siblings. People gathered to listen or judge or embellish the performance: local lads took up the rhythm, clapping and drumming, and made a complicated mosaic of sound; a trio of old men recaptured their youth singing in rusty tones to much acclaim; other lads shouted encouragement and the crowd echoed with whoops and whistles as some

---

* Travelling players have always been popular in Egypt and are the heirs of a long musical tradition of popular entertainment in the countryside and towns. Travelling musicians perform at weddings, Mulids (saints' days) and religious festivals. During Ramadan cafe owners often invite musicians to perform for customers after sunset when the fast is broken.

girls forgot themselves, alarming their chaperone, by a sudden round of prancing steps and a dangerous swishing of firmly-pinned veils. The old woman suppressed smiles and memories as the girls were herded out to the edge of the crowd with half-serious threats. The musician's tunes were capturing the different emotions of the people in the square.* But the old woman's pleasant thoughts subsided as she spied the troubled woman on her husband's arm, proudly parading her finery.

The wise old woman had been watching for some time, sensing the wickedness at work long before the prying eyes of neighbouring women had confirmed her worst fears. She was a wise one, familiar with the hosts of spirits which inhabit humans. She knew the spirits which take possession of people: the demons beneath the skin which choke women's instincts and natural feelings, leaving them powerless to resist. The old woman knew all this because of course she was mistress of the Zar ceremony.† She also knew about music because she led the musicians of the Zar who entice and entrap the spirits, so that she could loosen their grip on afflicted women. The wise woman knew about the power unleashed by different rhythmical patterns, a power which is unpredictable, therefore dangerous.

Remember that the spirits are enraged by some tunes as

---

* The musician is playing a traditional instrument called Rababa. This is a single-stringed type of violin often used to accompany heroic tales and love songs. The Rababa is played with a horsehair bow and in expert hands it produces a wonderful range of sounds. The Rababa can be particularly stirring when accompanied by Sigat (brass cymbals) and Darabuka (a type of large earthenware drum covered with skin at one end and open at the other).

† The Zar is a communal ceremony for the placation of spirits (afarit). The ifrit (spirit) is thought to enter the person's body when she (men are almost never possessed) is most vulnerable, for instance at night, after childbirth, in the toilet, when washing, or, as in this tale, when the victim is close to murky water, the home of some spirits. The Quran describes spirits as typifying 'the hidden forces and capacities of mankind' (Sura 55:15). Zar meetings have a leader who is known as Hakima (wise woman) or Sheikha (literally, a woman from a holy or learned family, but in this context it is often just a

surely as they are placated by others. The danger in music
is its effect on our emotions and that is much the same for
demons. The woman possessed by the demon of luxury
stood listening to the music. The travelling musician had
been joined by several others with drums and pipes and
tambourines. They were playing fast, fiery folk tunes,
dance music which conjured up images of the near-
forgotten village past of these city dwellers. Indeed, those
who were not dancing or singing or clapping seemed lost
in deep thought as if they were back in the homelands of
their ancestors. The woman swayed from side to side, not
in time to the music, but following some other deeper
rhythm in response to a force stirring within. The wise old
woman saw this and her heart grew cold. The people
beside the woman ignored her, caught up in the mood the
musicians created but also accustomed to overlooking the
excesses of her behaviour.

The demon was captivated by the furious drumming
and the swirling pipes and the shivering strings. It was
delighted with the first musician who led the band. His
bow moved faster, his top notes were higher, his low notes
more resonant, his rhythms more entrancing. The musician played on and on. The sweat fell from his brow like
huge raindrops as he put all his talent and skill into this
tune. The musician's expert bow flew across the violin. He
produced cries of pain, howls of agony, exclamations of
fear and fury, sudden whimpers and moans, then a
glorious explosion of laughter. On and on he played, faster
and faster. He was lost in the music of his own creation,
far from this crowded city square. He was under a cruel
desert sun playing for a little girl who haunted him from a

---

respectful title implying knowledge and wisdom), who has become familiar
with the spirit world by triumphing over a spirit which has possessed her. The
Zar musicians include players of drums, cymbals and tambourines who set
dance rhythms at Zar ceremonies. A woman is able to 'placate' the spirit which
possesses her by dancing to the point of exhaustion to a particular rhythm
which 'pleases' the spirit.

half-remembered dream. He fought the incomprehensible feeling of terror which always accompanied such memories. The musician feared that he might go mad and scream out: 'God of mercy help her, save her! Help me, save me!' A blood-chilling scream cut through the music, but it was not his.

The demon is revealed, it has shown itself. A woman throws herself on the ground, writhing, ripping her hair, tearing her gorgeous dress. Now she moans, now she wails, now mutters, now laughs with the horrible laughter of the insane.* The crowd forms a close circle around the woman: the latest attraction of the day. Some offer advice, others stand in helpless fascination. Is she mad, possessed, ill or merely seeking attention? The crowd's whispers fill the air and grow louder: 'Help her, bring her water, take her home, find the wise woman, get the pharmacist, she needs medicine, she needs a Sheikha, somebody do something to help her for God's sake!'

Now her husband and children are beside her, the man crouches down making hopeless attempts to calm his wife. She snarls at him and screams and her children draw back terrified. Indeed, it is quite clear that the demon has been forced to reveal its presence.

The old woman pushes people aside and a message flows through the crowd that the wise one is coming. A small group of women follow, watching her every move and waiting for her instructions.† The woman is quiet now, she

---

* This type of behaviour is typical of women in the throes of spirit possession. Symptoms of possession may also include fainting fits, speaking in tongues and various types of self-destructive acts. When this happens in public, naturally it attracts a crowd of onlookers who openly debate whether the woman is actually possessed or just faking affliction for some personal end, such as obtaining one of the valuable gifts which jealous spirits tend to demand.

† A Hakima who leads a Zar group has a small group of helpers. These women share some of the wise women's knowledge of the spirits and assist her during Zar ceremonies. After the Zar leader's death, one of the assistants may inherit the role of Hakima and her personal Zar group following.

lies in the dust as if asleep. Her elaborate dress is soiled and torn beyond repair. She does not stir when her husband lifts her into his arms and follows after the wise woman. The possessed woman is put down on a bed roll in a tiny dark room full of mysterious smells. The old woman keeps this room perfumed with exotic secret oils which please the spirits. Now that the demon has shown itself it is weak and vulnerable in the wise woman's hands.

The wise woman concentrated her powers, forgetting the anxious husband, her attentive helpers, those who clustered outside on the doorstep, and even the woman herself. She began to hum and chant, sometimes in soft low tones, sometimes in wails and shrieks, but it was a constant, steady song, a song to entice the demon.

Outside the room, the musician stood with the curious onlookers and waited. These events were beyond his comprehension, but he sensed that he had played some part in the terrible thing that had passed. He could see the canal from the dream in his mind's eye and this image would not leave him. He imagined that he heard the little girl's awful laughter coming from the room. He could hear the unnatural churning water, the bubbling from murky depths. He did not stop to consider why, but reached for his bow to drown these sounds with others of his own making, he had to play. The demon was stirring again, hungry for sensation and keen to indulge itself. The demon desired the tantalising rhythm which had attracted it before. The sound of drumming and humming filled the wise woman's room.

The drum beats thudded and throbbed, the chanting rose and faded and rose again. The demon was attracted by all these patterns but none produced the ultimate sensation. All at once a distant rhythm floated into the room, a staccato bowing of luxurious chords which merged with the constant drumming. This music enchanted the senses and emotions of all who heard it. The demon was enticed by the elaborate rhythms and finally entrapped by them.

A sudden inhuman howl shredded the air as if a wild beast was being burned alive.

Afterwards, the old woman appeared in the doorway, behind her the man was helping his wife to her feet. He supported her carefully as they moved to the entrance of the house.

The woman was walking unsteadily, but now free of the demon, she seemed to have lost her love of attention and proud show. Now her eyes were clear and lowered in modesty. The woman pulled a scarf across her face and left the house on her husband's arm.*

The crowd muttered with relief that this terrible thing was over. They did not notice the musician slumped against a wall. He seemed worn out and asleep on his feet, but his face had lost its haunted look. The musician was too exhausted to be fully aware that his extravagant music had brought the demon forth into the grasp of the wise woman, but the images of the little girl engulfed by evil by the canal no longer haunted him.

The following morning gave the promise that it would turn out to be a very fine day. A woman had just woken with a smile on her face as if from a long untroubled sleep. She stared around her in wonder. She dressed quickly with no concern for proud show and looked out of the window. To her unclouded eyes the sky seemed like a shimmering blue gem and the bright sun was a brilliant diamond. Turning back to the room, she smiled again in simple joy at the drowsy faces of her children. They were more precious,

---

* There are many tales which describe how a woman's modesty is restored as soon as a demon of possession is driven out. A good example of this is provided by the tale of the Forty-Seventh Night from the classic tale cycle the *Arabian Nights*: 'The king sent for his daughter and they brought her in bound and fettered. The Holy Man made her sit behind a curtain and taking out the hairs from her head, burned them and fumigated her with the smoke. At that moment he who was in her head cried out and departed from her. She instantly recovered her sanity, and veiling her face at once, asked, "What has happened to me?"'

more beautiful and more dear to her heart than anything else in the world.

Oum Idris kept up her customary commentary throughout the tale, although perhaps she was less vicious in her condemnation of the central character's flaws and more generous in her praise of the happy conclusion than usual. Everyone agreed that it was a wonderful tale and Oum Idris echoed these sentiments without the typically ambiguous flattery she tends to reserve for a successful storyteller. She also spoke with great sincerity about the importance of storytelling as a way of airing grievances and excorcising society's demons. Instead of her expected barbed comment on departing, the women exchanged meaningful looks when Oum Idris thanked the storyteller a second time. Her final remark was that 'an excellent tale is always worth hearing because it makes you feel better inside'.

Traditional folk tales are told in the storytelling circle from time to time. There is a rich store of tales in the local oral tradition known to all from childhood. Most mothers have told the stories to their children at home and everyone enjoys listening to them again in the company of other women and children. Some women have a particular favourite which they request, others are happy to let the storyteller choose. Oum Mohammed is the acknowledged expert when it comes to telling folk tales. She narrated the following version of one of the most popular stories.

THE PRINCESS AND THE PEARL MERCHANT

This is a tale of male stubbornness and misplaced pride. Women know that such things have all the force of thunder, but being more sound than substance it's true that they will pass as suddenly as a summer storm.

Once upon a time a beautiful princess was lost to the world. She looked as if she was in a deep sleep, but nobody could wake her and she had been like this for a very long time. This was no ordinary slumber or rest from the worries of the world, because it was an enchanted sleep. The princess's pulse was weak and her breathing was so shallow that it seemed as if she was about to die. What had happened? The truth is that her father, a rich and proud warrior king, had given her a terrible shock which made her heart falter. One day the princess had been amusing herself with some embroidery when her father announced: 'My daughter, my fair one, you are the jewel of my life and it is time for you to marry. I am going to find a husband for you.' The princess grew pale as her father continued, 'I have sent messages to all the princes of the world and they are going to come to the palace one by one until I find the most suitable man best matched to our wealth and nobility.'

You might think that these words would have delighted the princess, but they had quite the opposite result. No sooner had her father paused for breath than she fell into a dead faint. The great warrior king was as helpless as a baby as he stood over his unconscious daughter not knowing what to do. First he tried patting her cheek, as nervous as a boy with a wild horse. Then he stroked her hair gently and whispered her name, begging her to open her eyes. Then he prodded her with a cautious finger as if afraid that she might jump up and bite him. In the end, at a loss, he called for the keeper of the princess's chamber, her personal maidservant. This wise old woman watched over the litter bearers as they carried the princess to her bedroom on a silver litter. As for the distraught father, she left the matter in the hands of the chief overseer of the palace servants.

When the old woman had laid the princess on the bed she saw that there was nothing more to be done. The princess was in a deep sleep and could not be disturbed. The maidservant discussed the catastrophe with the palace overseer. 'What can be wrong with the princess?' the overseer wondered aloud. 'It is a great mystery, but I have sent for the greatest experts in the kingdom and one of them will find a cure. In the end all will be well with God's help.' The wise old maidservant said nothing because she knew that the princess could not be cured by all the spell-workers and magicians and masters of the spirits in the world. She had been the princess's closest companion since her mother, the good queen, had died and there were few secrets between them. The old servant knew the true cause of the princess's trance-like state.

During the following weeks the experts arrived at the palace and examined the sleeping princess. Some pricked her fingers with silver pins until there were drops of blood on the fine white sheets, but the princess did not wake. Some bathed her with powerful magic lotions, but although the pungent aromas made people's eyes water, they did not wake the princess. The experts tried many types of cure. Charms and spells were chanted, special spices were placed between her lips, delicate music was played to charm the spirits which might be making the girl sleep, but each new magic remedy was as useless as the last. The Great Sultan of Baghdad's renowned magician ground diamonds and emeralds into tiny particles and sprinkled the princess with the precious powder, but she did not stir. The most famous royal physician burned peacock tails under the princess's nose, but even he experienced his first failure when she did not recover.

The warrior king grew angry as his fears for his daughter increased. His promises of rewards grew ever louder and more generous. His declaration:'I will give one hundred gold pieces to the one who wakes the princess' was replaced by: 'I will give one thousand gold pieces'. Finally, he pronounced: 'I will give ten thousand!' But money was not enough to inspire the experts or to guarantee their success. However hard they tried, the princess remained lost to the world.

One year passed and the princess had not stirred once in her enchanted slumber. The great warrior king grew old and weak as he watched over her. He felt that part of his life was lost with each new day of her decline. The princely flock of would-be husbands came to the palace full of high hopes. Each prince was eager to be chosen as the husband of such a wealthy princess. For one thing they were all thrilled by the sleeping girl's beauty, for another, they admired her silent condition as if this was indeed the most perfect quality a wife could possess. Each proud prince begged the king to let him marry the princess and vowed to take good care of her until she awoke. But the king saw through their schemes, and each time one of them tried to negotiate a marriage deal (arranging for a reduction in wedding gifts, of course, on account of her enchantment), the king refused with all the politeness he could muster.

Seven days and nights after the first anniversary of the princess's sleep, the king sent his sons on a final mission to find an expert who would wake her. The four young men, all brave warriors, rode off into the far corners of the realm. Seven days later, three had returned alone with the news that not one expert sage remained who had not visited the palace already. The youngest son was the last to ride into the palace courtyard on his fine stallion, behind him followed an ancient man wearing tattered robes and dusty sandals. The young prince introduced him as a wandering wise man who had offered to try to cure the princess. The king welcomed him graciously. The assembled people of the court were shocked at the sight of such a beggar. But the warrior king was a man of his word. He offered the poor old man the same astonishing reward as the famous magicians and royal physicians had been promised should he wake the princess.

The dervish (for this was the true identity of the one who looked like an ancient beggar) went to the sleeping princess's bedside and watched her intently. Her breathing was slow and shallow. He took her smooth creamy arm and felt her pulse, which was weak and regular. The room was full of experts, royal physicians, eminent magicians and the like, and they all watched the dervish with suspicion. Their elaborate cures had been unsuccessful, so they were bound to doubt the skills of the poor old tramp and wonder at the sanity of a king who permitted such a man to touch a noble-born princess.

The dervish bent over the girl and held her hand as he began to whisper a string of words in a low monotonous voice. The experts looked at each other in mock surprise. This was not a great spell of fine mysterious words, the old fool was simply reciting the names of great cities! 'Cairo,' whispered the dervish, 'Damascus.' He paused after each word and checked the girl's pulse, but there was no reaction. The dervish concentrated harder. 'Beirut,' he whispered but the heartbeat of the princess remained slow and regular. 'Baghdad,' he whispered. No reaction. 'Samarkand.' No sooner had he said the word than the princess's pulse made a sudden leap and her heart fluttered in her breast like a small bird in a cage. The dervish paused for a moment and called: 'Your majesty, a little progress I think, beg the scribe to record Samarkand.'

The ancient man ignored the murmurs of disbelief and incomprehension and bent his feeble body over the princess so that he could whisper into her delicate ear once more. The people of the court strained to hear what madness he would whisper this time. The dervish began with 'Gold,' but he sensed no change in the sleeping princess. 'Copper,' he whispered, 'Silk, silver, diamonds, rubies.' None of these words provoked the quickening of her pulse that he was expecting. Then he tried 'Amber, frankincense, ivory.' Nothing. But as soon as he said 'Pearls,' he felt her pulse leap under his fingertips. 'Your Majesty,' he said, 'a little more progress, there is a certain pearl merchant in the city of Samarkand, please ask the scribe to record: Pearl Merchant from Samarkand.'

At this point the king could contain his feelings no longer. 'What is all this nonsense!' he demanded. 'What is the point of your riddles? In God's name restore my daughter to her senses. Samarkand has many pearl merchants but how will this help my daughter to regain her sanity!' 'Patience, great King' said the dervish. 'All will be known in time.'

All this time the wise old chambermaid had been watching from the servants' quarters. Her own heart had jumped with each word the dervish proclaimed. She understood what these things meant more than the court experts who were trying to look wise and superior and acting as if the dervish was an obvious fool. The whispers began again. 'Thin, fat, short, bald, rich.' The princess did not stir, her breast rose and fell with the gentle movements of a sleeping child. Then the dervish said, 'Tall, dark and handsome.' The princess made a little jump and her eyelashes fluttered. 'Ah, yes, yes,' muttered the dervish. 'Your Majesty, we are progressing very well, very well indeed. Scribe, please write that there is a tall, dark, handsome pearl merchant in the city of Samarkand.' This statement was greeted with astonished silence.

'What!' thundered the king at last. 'Tell me his name. I will kill him with my bare hands if he has touched a hair of my daughter's head or harmed her in any way.' 'Patience, O King' said the dervish, 'I will find out his name. Remember, all will be known in time.' The dervish bent over the princess again and whispered, 'Mohammed, Mahmud, Issak, Ibrahim.' No reaction. 'Tahir, Talib, Yussef, Yunus.' Still no reaction. 'Omar, Akbar, Ahmed.' At the last name the princess sighed and smiled and opened her eyes. 'The name you want is Ahmed,' said the dervish. 'Scribe, write down that there is a tall, dark, handsome pearl dealer called Ahmed who lives in . . .'

'Enough!' roared the king. 'Who is this man and what has he to do with my daughter?' The dervish let go the princess's hand and said, 'You should ask your daughter yourself, O King. The princess is awake now!' The people of the court gasped as the princess sat up, stretching her arms, yawning and smiling as if she had just awakened from a refreshing nap. The king was overjoyed and rushed over to embrace his daughter. He spoke softly but forcefully. 'Your secret has been revealed, my dear one, but you must tell me about this man Ahmed the pearl merchant, what has he done to you my darling daughter?' The princess smiled a secretive smile and said nothing. She yawned and sighed, looking for all the world as if she was about to close her eyes and fall asleep again. The king grew more insistent. 'Tell me at once,' he urged, 'who is this man and what is he to you?'

'Ahmed, the pearl merchant from Samarkand, came to the palace last year.' The old maidservant spoke and her words seemed to shake the new veil of sleep which was falling over the princess. The princess smiled again at the mention of his name. The king turned to the old maid. 'What do you know of the matter?' he demanded. She stepped forward and bowed her head. She said, 'Your majesty, the merchant Ahmed supplied the finest pearls in the world here at your command in this very palace. You said that the pearls which he put on your daughter's dress were like a thousand bright stars.' The king's eyes narrowed as he searched for some memory of the merchant. 'Tell me more, tell me everything, old servant!' he commanded. The old woman answered, 'My lord, I can only tell you this as a mere servant whose life depends on your protection. My mistress must tell you the rest in her own words, Sire.'

'Dearest father, my servant speaks the truth about Ahmed the pearl merchant from Samarkand,' the princess said. She looked serene and her eyes shone when she said the name of her beloved. Indeed this was the secret she had shared with her faithful maidservant. The princess continued her story with increasing passion. 'Father, you must know that I am in love with the good merchant who came to the palace last year. He chose his very best pearls for me at your request, and he helped the dressmakers to position them on my gown. When we saw each other we fell in love at once. Each time our eyes met across the room

I knew for certain that he was the man I wanted to marry. After his return to Samarkand I wanted to mention the matter to you but I was afraid. Then when you announced that the parade of fine suitors was to begin I was heart-broken. I will die if I cannot marry my true love, Ahmed the pearl merchant.'

The great warrior king was outraged. 'What nonsense,' he roared. 'You are a foolish girl full of childish notions, what can you know about suitable husbands! The daughter of a great king cannot marry a pearl merchant and that's an end to it! You must marry a rich man who will keep you in a palace, not in a bazaar store. You must have lush gardens to stroll in, not a patch of rough grass in front of a poor man's hovel. A rich husband will provide the finest food and jewels and fabrics. What will your pearl merchant provide to compare with all this? What ridiculous ideas you girls have!'

The king was content that his strong words had changed the princess's mind. But the princess was the daughter of a proud line of warriors and she replied with equally strong words. 'Dearest father, what are fine palaces and lush gardens and elaborate gowns without love? Can riches make love bloom? Can riches cure the sick and wake the dead? I will die if I cannot marry Ahmed the pearl merchant.' The princess spoke with great self-assurance, then closed her eyes and lay down as if prepared to sleep forever.

The king was shaken by the strength of his daughter's words. He turned to the dervish in despair. 'Tell me what to do, old man,' he said, 'you revealed my daughter's secret and brought her back to life, now tell me how to make her happy.' The dervish simply smiled and answered, 'My Lord, the princess herself has given you the remedy.' The king was moved to anger and snapped, 'But the idea is ridiculous, a pearl merchant can't marry a princess. Tell me how to cure the princess of this mad passion!' The dervish smiled a second mysterious smile and replied, 'My Lord, I know of only three cures for true love: death,

insanity or marriage.' By now the king was very angry. He
was determined to get rid of the dervish before he made
him seem even more foolish with his riddles and cryptic
comments.

'Old man, you have done enough,' the king said, 'take
your reward for waking the princess and go home.' The
dervish bowed and said, 'I ask for no reward other than the
happiness of the princess.' The king was puzzled. 'Do you
refuse the ten thousand gold pieces which I have offered
to anyone who would cure my daughter?' The dervish
nodded, then shook his head and looked very mysterious:
'I do not refuse your reward my Lord, but neither do I ask
for anything for myself.'

The king turned away to hide his confusion and noticed
that the chambermaid was at her mistress's bedside. 'Stop
her from falling asleep, save her from this terrible insanity,
old woman,' he begged. The old woman replied, 'I can do
nothing, master, the matter is not in my hands.' The king
suddenly lost his temper. 'Do you think the matter is in my
hands then! What can I do?' he bellowed. The old servant
bowed very low but did not answer. She went over and said
something to the dervish without looking at the king, who
was growing even more furious. 'Stop this nonsense at
once!' he shouted in a voice like thunder which shook the
curtains. 'What are you ancient ones whispering about?'

The dervish answered for them both: 'O King, with
your gracious permission I would like to accept my reward
and leave your great palace.' The king had a huge trunk
of gold brought into the room and breathed a sigh of relief,
at least one of his problems would be solved with the
curious old man's departure. 'Old woman, have you anything to add to this?' the king asked slyly, not expecting
an answer. The old woman bowed very low and said, 'I beg
your forgiveness, Sire, but I can only repeat that this matter has nothing to do with me. I will spend my last days caring for the sleeping princess as your humble servant.' She

went back to the bed where the princess lay and began to rearrange the cushions and covers.

The great warrior king was distraught, having forgotten about his daughter in the heat of the moment. He ran to her bedside. 'Dearest one, stay awake, fight against this affliction, don't leave me,' he begged. The princess stared at him sadly through half-closed eyes. 'Father, I will die if I cannot marry Ahmed the pearl merchant. If I cannot be his wife I would rather fade from this world than live without him,' she sighed. 'It is impossible, this Ahmed is a poor man,' the king protested sadly, realising how hollow the words sounded after his daughter's passionate pleas. 'My dearest, you cannot be this man's wife, he is just an ordinary merchant with no more than a hundred gold pieces to his name. For your sake I wish it could be different.'

'But my Lord,' the dervish said quietly, 'Ahmed the pearl merchant now has more than ten thousand gold pieces.' The king was astonished. 'How can this be?' he demanded. The ancient dervish pointed to the vast trunk which contained the fortune in gold. 'Remember my reward,' he said. 'I asked for nothing for myself, only that the princess's happiness be restored.'

For once the great warrior king was defeated, first by the power of true love and then by the wisdom of the aged. These things considered, how could he object? He relented at once and sent a messenger to Samarkand to bring back Ahmed, the tall, dark, handsome pearl merchant who would marry his daughter. The young merchant came to the palace and the power of love fully restored his beautiful bride's health and happiness. There was a great wedding feast which lasted seven days and nights and God blessed the couple with a long and happy life and the gift of many sons.

OUM MOHAMMED: A TRIUMPHANT WOMAN

Oum Mohammed is the most frequent hostess and a familiar storyteller. She takes considerable pride in her social skills and hospitality. On the occasions when the women do not meet in her spare room she still acts as hostess and greets the others as they arrive. She is freely accorded the prestigious status of old and respected woman at every private or public social event. Oum Mohammed lowers her corpulent frame on to the low stool which accompanies her everywhere. This sets her apart from the others and ensures that she occupies the highest position in the room since everyone else sits on the floor. She is an expert listener, a likely accompaniment to being a skilled storyteller. She always seems to know when an atmospheric exclamation or a sudden sigh is needed to enrich and embellish a tale. Her perception of the emotional forces unleashed by a tale is perfectly tuned. This may be a result of the wealth of experience she has acquired during her long, eventful life. Oum Mohammed chose to describe her life in the following way.

Like my father and his father before him, our family has always lived here next to the mosque. That mosque has seen everything that's happened to me in my life, the good and bad and the joy and the sorrow, and it hasn't collapsed. I'm as solid as that old building, believe me, an earthquake wouldn't demolish me! I have been married three times and the contracts were signed within those walls. After my two divorces I wept there, and the stones were as hard and dry as the heart of a cruel man. I prayed to God for my sick husband there before he died, God protect his soul. I sought blessing there in that mosque before every child of mine came into the world. As I said, the mosque has seen everything in my life. You should ask it for my story!

I am more than eighty years old now and they say I'm the oldest person hereabouts. Maybe I'm the oldest woman ever in this neighbourhood, for we have to lead a hard life by God's will. Still, I'm strong and healthy, thanks be to God. Now even my first-born son and the girl after him are dead, and my two youngest sons are the only ones with much spirit left in them. But my family is such a joy to me and my sons are the pride of my life. I am lucky with my children and have been blessed with a large family. I have given birth to more than twenty children and I'm proud of the size of my family. Some children died before they grew up and two adult sons are dead now. But I don't see all my children together very often. The girls all found good husbands and that is where their duty lies now. A women's children are her greatest blessing. Where would I be, old as I am, without my sons to look after me?

I have had a long and busy life and of course I've had my share of sorrow. These bad things seemed to strike at my heart as sudden and indiscriminate as a snake. But just one old memory of my children sleeping or my sons playing in the street can lift me out of the depression. My sons Ehab and Ahmed are such a joy to me. I live here with Ehab and his wife and my grandchildren. You see I am in the cradle of good care and family protection. Ahmed, who lives close by, has his wife make sweets for me every Friday. At feast times we all share meals together. They are the kind of sons any woman would be proud of.

My family is all in the city around me, they have married well and are happy and comfortable, with fine children of their own. I made sure that each one found a good partner. When a marriage goes wrong there is always trouble and pain and hardship. I know this too well. When my children were growing up I was determined to protect them from the kind of marriage problems that I'd experienced, though bad luck was behind much of that.

Thinking back, I suppose that you could say my first three daughters were the cause of my first divorce. You see, my first husband wasn't a patient man and he wouldn't wait for me to give him a son. That was a hard time for me. I thought that I might die of the shame of divorce, especially when I knew people might say that I was cursed never to have sons. I almost believed it myself because my husband didn't seem able to talk about anything else at the time! He was not a good man and I soon realised that I was better off without him.

After the divorce I was in great distress and in the terrible position where I had to fend for myself and take care of the children alone. Of course I was far from hopeless and all was not lost! I married again within a few months, this time to a cousin on my father's side of the family. My first husband was a cousin too, but a more distant one from my mother's side. People in this area have great faith in marriage with cousins, and naturally it's good to be married to someone who is loyal to your family through common blood. Still, I've come to think that any good stranger is at least as safe a bet as a bad relative!

Kalif, this second husband of mine, was my youngest paternal cousin. He was about the same age as me and seemed a nice young man when we married. He helped my father and brothers to collect all my things back after the first divorce. You could say that Kalif was like a son to my father and both of them were happy with the marriage; one was taking me off the other's hands. At the time I was happy too because I had all my furniture and cooking things back, as well as my fabrics and trinkets and so on. I never lost sight of my gold wedding gifts, I was lucky with that first divorce, so that wasn't a problem! There I was, a wife again, and this time I was a little wiser. This husband was a good man, I thought, he will be nice to me and treat me well and I will have sons for him. Of course it was a good deal for Kalif too, remember that he had a ready-made home at no personal cost when I got my possessions back from the first marriage!

Once you're sure that everything is fine there is bound to be some unexpected disaster, and this stage of my life was no exception! There was a terrible sickness in this area soon after our wedding which lasted the whole month of Ramadan. It was a nightmare. Every member of my own family died at this terrible time, apart from my older sister. I was orphaned and deprived of my close kin within a matter of weeks. I felt like a tiny child again although I was a grown woman. My sister had been married for some years and had her own home, so I took over my parents' rooms. Oh yes, as a new wife I was even able to provide my husband with a roof and walls!

Kalif was annoyed by this but of course he couldn't let it show and he had nothing to complain about. Was it my fault that he had few material things to offer? He thought so. Still, as I said, he was in no position to change the balance of affairs and his feelings of inadequacy were his problem! He wasn't a rich man because his side of the family hadn't been very successful in the city. This didn't worry me at the time, but Kalif had bitter feelings buried inside. Indeed, I was only fully aware of this side of him much later on and then I began to understand the problems it had caused in our marriage.

Of course all men are like that, they're obsessed with showing the world how manly they are. Men love to boast that they gave their family this or that, and it cost this much, and their pockets are this deep! Foolish? Of course it is! If we have enough to eat, and can share things with our relatives and help other people, it doesn't matter who provides it. But men get depressed when they don't have money to show off, yet at the same time they complain that they have to exhaust themselves to earn money for the family! That's not a very well balanced argument! Still, to be fair, men don't have an easy life here either.

Thinking back to my second marriage, it's no lie to say that I was smarter than Kalif. I was a lot smarter than my first husband too, that almost goes without saying. In fact I can outwit any man! I'm not boasting about it, it's the truth. Of course women can and do outwit the men of their households. Most women can always get the better of their father, husband, brother and the rest, though many would die before they'd admit it! I'm able to talk like this and speak openly because I'm so old. If men overhear me they just laugh and call me a dear old fool.

I worked just as hard as any man during my younger years. I even watched over the stall that my second husband had. He sold hot food and snacks like pickles, ful beans and tamiyyah. I prepared the food in my own kitchen, so while he was the vendor I did more than a fair share of the work and earned more than half the money. In addition to keeping the home and housework, as Kalif's wife I made sure that I didn't neglect my other domestic duties. I gave Kalif eleven children in the years we were married, a son and a daughter time about. I cried with joy after every birth and it felt like the tears came from the very depths of me. The happiest tears followed the birth of each son. You remember the cause? I had six sons and it was as if God was showing how wrong my first husband had been.

In the years with Kalif we had little spare money and it grew worse with the birth of each child. There were too many open mouths and not enough spoonfuls to shut them. At times it was quite impossible to stretch out the little food we had so everyone had something to eat. I admit that occasionally I ended up weeping and hungry as well as miserable. I used to give my dinner to the boys and silence my grumbling stomach with water, but I never wasted energy on tears for long. I tried to use my talents in the kitchen to make a little go a long way. Perhaps this is the best gift a woman can have in a world of hardship. My own mother had thirteen children and she taught me well.

A good wife needs to know how to make a meal out of the poorest ingredients and waste nothing. It was the first thing I looked for in the girls my sons were to marry. There can be endless problems between a mother and her sons' wives, as well as petty fights and jealousy, but there's nothing like that under this roof. We both love the same men, one side as a wife, the other as a mother. They are

responsible for my sons' comfort and happiness, and sometimes it's not that different from looking after the children.
My daughters-in-law are finishing the job I started and
perhaps it's even more difficult now that my sons are men.
I chose my sons' wives well and I know they are good
wives. They are respectful to their husbands' mother, and
that's a very important thing indeed.

When I think about my life in general I remember a lot
of things which centred on the question of money. People
here all do, especially the women. We always end up
talking about money; too little and there's heartache, too
much and it's still the same. The worst time I had was
when my last child to Kalif was just a few months old. We
never had enough to eat and there were continual fights
and squabbles about money. Then everything changed. It
seemed like a gift from God when my husband inherited
a small store after his uncle's death. I thought that this was
the solution to all our problems. Of course this luck turned
out to be more like an act of the devil.

One day soon after this inheritance Kalif called me away
from the laundry tub and told me that he was taking
another wife. Just like that, just when I had dared to dream
of the extra money that would make our life more comfortable after years of hardship! I'll never forget that day as
long as I live. I remember it as clearly as yesterday. My
soapy hands were dripping water all over the best bed
cover. Time had stopped and I was frozen to the spot. It
was as if I had grown roots and would stand there for ever,
saying nothing, just dripping soap suds like an old sheet
on a washing line. He told me all about the girl he wanted
to marry and sounded happy and excited. He was relieved
that I appeared to take this news so well. Of course he was
stupid enough to believe that my silence meant that I was
as overjoyed as he evidently was! I felt like murdering them
both, but I wasn't that stupid.

Nadia, the girl he wanted to marry, was fifteen years old
and I knew her as a child who had played with my own

daughters. Despite my pain and shock it occurred to me
that I had been one year younger than her on my own wedding day. I also knew that she was not as smart as I had
been then! But I accepted what he announced that awful
day, what else could I do? I said nothing, no wailing or
protests or threats, I just made plans. I used my brains and
waited. When he brought her to the house I even felt
sorry for her, but not much! From the very start I refused
to help her in any way because I believe that all women
have to learn to please their husbands by themselves.
Nadia cooked for him and burned the food and she rinsed
his clothes in dirty water. Clearly her mother had taught
her nothing at all.

As I said, I waited and watched. My plan was to make
Kalif divorce me. If he was foolish enough to want to marry
this stupid child and expect me to be a co-wife with her,
then he would be foolish enough to divorce me. Of course
it wasn't that easy. Although Kalif was quite drunk with
pride on account of his new young wife, he still had some
ability to think. He also was greedy and well aware of the
economic cost of divorcing me. He was living in my rooms
with my possessions around, and had cheerfully squan-
dered his inheritance money on his new bride without
a thought for the future. But God is good and everything
went my way in the end.

Before long Kalif and Nadia were making such a spectacle of their romance that everyone was outraged. It was
quite disgusting and even Kalif's family criticised him,
although they blamed the child bride! His stupidity with
the inheritance money and his profligate ways made their
presence intolerable. The two of them finally packed their
few possessions and left the area. The children and I stayed
here with everything we needed in my hands again. It was
a sweet victory. I got my divorce and didn't care about
maintenance payments, I was just happy he was out of my
life. You see, all that time when I was waiting patiently, I
saved what I could and planned for the day when I would

be alone again. I even sold some of my gold jewellery, though it broke my heart. But there are times when women have to do this, after all jewellery is a woman's greatest source of future security. We have to use it in times of greatest need. So the gold bracelets from my first marriage kept the family fed. No woman ever forgets that her survival shines and jingles on her wrists.

After this difficult experience I had to face something even worse. I had to find a way of earning more money because I had no husband and the children were still growing. For a while we all did something to bring in money, from the very youngest to the oldest. The older boys were already working. One worked with the vegetable seller and he brought home damaged goods which helped fill out our meal. Another worked for the tailor and he supplied odd scraps of fabric which kept us clothed, or at least well mended and patched. The little ones came to the food stall with me. Imagine that, imagine me working in the streets!

But of course I didn't find it shameful, although I hated having to work in such a low and exposed job. I had to make money to eat and I wasn't innocent of this experience, hadn't I worked before when times were hard? More important, what mother would watch her children starve for the sake of pride and worry about what people might say? I'd cut my own veins first. In fact instead of slander or criticism I found that people seemed friendlier than ever. Everyone wished me well and offered all kinds of favours when they saw how I loved my family and was prepared to suffer any indignity to see them provided for.

After a year of toiling like a man, I met my next husband. From this point in time I can say for certain that he was the kind of man I wish I'd married when I was fourteen. But in those days I had no intention of going through any more heartache with a new husband. Well, this man Mohammed started coming to my stall every day. He bought enough pickles and sandwiches to feed three men! He always made a fuss of the children and played with

them, and then friends told me that he had been heard
asking about me in the area. This was a crucial piece of
news. Mohammed was asking lots of local people about
me, even though I knew who he was and he knew all about
me because he lived in the next district. However, this is
an important way of approaching the issue of marriage.
Mohammed certainly was making his interest in me public
knowledge.

Mohammed was a fine man. When I first came to know
him he was a tailor working from a room in his cousin's
home. He had been living there since he came to the city.
I knew that he had been married before, but his wife had
died in childbirth a long time ago. People said that he had
been stricken with grief for years. As far as I could see it
was a perfect situation, at last I had a chance to marry a
good man. If you can think of him from my point of view
you'll understand why I started to see the point of being
a wife again. There he was, a big, strong man with a reputation for hard work, and there I was, alone with my
children in the midst of hardship. Well, even a fool could
recognise the advantages!

After a few months I'd made up my mind. I didn't think
twice and decided to marry him immediately. Neither of
us had close kin and so the wedding arrangements were
simple and swift. The marriage contract was the shortest
one I'd ever had, and the best. Mohammed agreed to live
in my home after I had announced that I would never leave
it, and I haven't! The place had been empty of a man
for too long and I was overjoyed to fill it with a good one.
We had such happy years together. There was enough
money to live comfortably and the children were well cared
for.

It often seems that a woman has to suffer before she
earns the right to happiness, and money, or the lack of it,
always brings unhappiness to a marriage. Money is like a
knife with two sharp edges, a scarcity causes fights and
trouble for the wife, and an over-abundance makes the

man a dreamer and fills his head with madness for a new wife.

I knew the last situation well from my own experience, just think how Kalif turned out. But this time it was different, Mohammed and I had just enough money to be happy and secure. During our happy years together I gave Mohammed ten children, and I was indeed blessed because seven of them were sons. One of the greatest gifts that a woman can have must be the birth of twin boys, and this happened to me twice. My husband had been a twin but his brother had died young, so we named the first set of twins Mohammed and Hussein after their father and the much-mourned uncle the boys would never meet.

It was around this time that another dark cloud settled over my life. I started to suffer from vicious pains in my legs and back and I'm still troubled by them. I was in great distress because the pain was so severe and I tried everything to find a cure. Some people said that the pain was a result of working in the street when I had to stand all day and do a man's job. But I felt that the illness was a result of the Evil Eye and knew that I was cursed with the pain. I was sure that the evil was coming from Nadia, the girl my second husband married. The main problem was that Kalif's pride and greed had turned his brain inside-out. As he grew old he had become like a young lad who wants everything he looks at. Another young wife had replaced Nadia before too long, so she had suffered a divorce herself. I knew she blamed me for it, although you would have to be mad to think I was responsible. Did I try to stop them getting married! I also knew that Nadia was jealous of my large and happy family and miraculous fate to be the mother of so many sons.

Once I realised that Nadia was the source of the evil I didn't need further proof. I could feel the evil in my bones and what could be greater proof than that! I knew that Nadia had bought a bad spell that was eating away my bones inside me and I've fought against her evil ever since.

I don't like to mention this outside because I have a feeling that evil spells and curses increase each time people talk about them, but I pray and have charms to protect myself. Over the years I've consulted many women who possess secret knowledge, but without success. I've visited wise women who know about such things but they haven't found a cure either. Even my sister, the greatest of all the wise women, can do nothing.* She told me that evil which comes from the hatred of this kind of woman is too strong to be broken. Nadia is perhaps a little mad herself now. People say that she speaks to no one and walks the streets not caring who sees her. But I have learned to live with the pain and have too many other things to be grateful for to let it upset me.

As I have said, they were happy years with Mohammed and both of us were blessed by the chance to see all our children engaged and married, and start new branches of their father's line. Of all the children, Mohammed's remain the closest to me in my last years. Mohammed was the best of fathers to all the children, even those from my other marriages. The sons who had gone to their own father's kin came to regard him as a favoured uncle, even though they shared no common blood. When Ehab, the first son of my second husband, came back here, he worked with Mohammed alongside his two half-brothers and they all grew strong and loyal as they worked together.

From the first day of our marriage I vowed that I would never work in the streets again, and Mohammed promised that he would always be a true husband and care for his household. Mohammed was not strong enough to do much

---

* Oum Mohammed's closest friend is the local Hakima, sometimes addressed as Sheikha, a renowned worker of spells. Oum Mohammed and the Sheikha consider themselves as close as if they were from the same family and call each other 'my sister'. Fictive kinship (addressing a non-relative as sister, brother, cousin, etc.) is a common way of stressing intimate and highly valued personal relationships. This is especially important given the high value placed on family ties and the sense of isolation people feel when migration removes them from a wide circle of village kin.

work during the last few years of our life together in this world. But he was content to let his fine sons take care of the business and he could rest safe in the knowledge that we were all well provided for. When he died, I mourned like a teenage widow.

Throughout his illness I watched him suffer and grow weaker and knew that death gave him peace from pain. I will never cease to grieve for him until death reunites us again.

In spite of my grief for Mohammed's death, I am a content old woman. My family is large and strong enough to give me the support an old woman needs near the end of her days. As old and as wise as I am, I never thought that I would be so well provided for in my last years, or so full of my own spirit and love of life. More than anyone I know, my life proves an important thing about women: that we can triumph in our struggle with men. I eventually succeeded in finding a fine husband and bearing many sons, and my sense of triumph lies in those bonds which fill you with joy and pride.

There were many special occasions when women had reason to spice the communal gathering with a spirit of celebration. Oum Mohammed's birthday was unquestionably the most special and celebratory of such occasions. Her sister-in-law, another storyteller and woman of high status, was the hostess that evening. Oum Mohammed's arrival was met with cheers and a flood of good wishes. There were special cakes and the expensive sweets which she adores. All the women had scrimped on the family food budget to provide these treats; even Oum Karim, the very poorest of all these poor women, had bought a huge bag of luxurious sugar-coated nuts. Oum Mohammed did not miss this and was lavish in her thanks, which quite embarrassed Oum Karim. There was little preliminary gossip or chat after the tea was served. All the women knew that the evening's tale would be the highlight of all the tributes which could be paid to Oum Mohammed. It was Oum Mohammed's Great Day in all respects, particularly in the telling of the tale itself.

THE WISE OLD CAT

This is a tale of triumph over hardship. It is a tale of a life well lived and a well deserved reward. Wit and wisdom are the virtues at the heart of the tale.

Once there was a fine cat who sat on a fine cushion. The cat was old and wise and deserved its life of luxury and ease. It had not always been so blessed with good things. The wise old cat was well known, well loved and respected in its home district. The cat loved its home and knew every inch of the area. It knew where the best scraps were to be found. It knew the best people and the worst people. There was nothing that the wise old cat did not know.

It knew a great deal about its neighbours' lives, things that they might have preferred to keep hidden, but nothing was hidden from the wise old cat. The cat rejoiced with its neighbours over good things, wept with them over sad things, and was not afraid to say harsh things when there was need of them. Nobody had a secret which the cat had not heard. Everyone looked up to the cat and wished they had as much wit and wisdom. The cat was generous, friendly and kind as well as being wise and clever. Some of these virtues were the result of its fine family background, but others had been acquired during its long, eventful life.

When the cat was young it was said to be one of the prettiest kittens ever seen. When the time came its parents wanted to find a fine husband to marry and take care of their little one. There were plenty of offers since the kitten was so pretty, and of course a decision was soon made. Everything in life is uncertain and the best decisions in the world are often the wrong ones. In short the fine husband was not such a fine man. He was no wiser than a donkey and before long he had abandoned the little cat and cast her out into the street.

This was a terrible time. Imagine the first experience of sorrow and remember that it is especially bitter when life appears to promise good things, as it always does. But such things are a challenge and a test of our nature. Such experiences offer a chance to learn how to cope with the world and how to make the best of ourselves. The little cat, who would become the wise old cat in the course of time, learned from this first experience of hardship. She vowed never to trust in male wisdom. The cat relied on her own strength and looked after herself and never forgot that male wisdom is a rare thing.

There were plenty of would-be husbands interested in the pretty cat, but the next one turned out no better than the first. This was a time of even greater sorrow and hardship because the cat was all alone in the world by then, not just abandoned by her first husband but also an orphan without a family to support her through difficulties. The second husband was no better than the first, maybe even worse, because he was greedy as well as stupid. This is a terrible combination indeed! But the cat struggled against every problem and found a solution.

The cat had her own kittens to consider now and she protected them with the fierce pride of a devoted mother. But the stupid, greedy husband was blind to all her efforts. While the cat managed to cope with the problems which confronted her, many caused by the lazy husband, and fought for scraps to feed her kittens, the husband looked around and grew greedy for a new mate. The poor cat was destined to be alone again, thrown back on her own resources. But this time she had known not to trust in male wisdom. The cat had observed the stupidity at work in her husband's mind. She did not make a fuss, but waited for the best moment to fight the greedy pair, and the wise cat had the final victory.

From this bitter experience the cat learned always to trust in her own judgement. She never forgot that a clear mind and a strong heart can outwit greed and stupidity.

In the difficult days ahead the cat suffered many things

for the sake of her kittens. The kittens were loved and cared for despite all the risks that this entailed. The cat had to do many unpleasant things. But she did not shirk this, because of her great love for her young family. Sometimes she had to fight for food in the streets. She had to behave in an undignified manner, which wounded her deeply. She had to take on the most aggressive opponents in a daily battle and use their own dirty tricks against them. None of this was pleasant but the cat did it to save her kittens. Naturally she grew even wiser and stronger.

From this experience the cat learned that while honour is not always found in obvious acts and words, honour and motherhood are always bound together. She never forgot this and grew even more respected the more people witnessed her devotion to the kittens.

It is curious how some creatures attract good fortune although few deserve it as much as this wise cat. Of course anyone who knows even a little of the cat's story will marvel at how wise and clever she was. Whatever the circumstances, the cat usually outwitted her enemies with her own clever tricks. However, there are some things which cannot be improved by clever plans alone, and in such cases the cat seemed to be aided by fortune. Those enemies who were not defeated by the cat herself appeared to fall victim to other forces. The cat led a charmed life and those who crossed her or wished her ill came to a bad end. If a cheat exploited the cat and emptied her purse with false promises, the cheat would fall into a ditch and lose the money he had obtained though deceit. If the cat was embarrassed by a vulgar beast which swore at her, the beast would lose its voice and was speechless the next time their paths crossed. Whoever slandered the cat or spread false gossip would suffer some shame of their own which kept tongues wagging for weeks to come. The stupid husband and the stupid, greedy husband both suffered and came to regret treating the cat so badly. The first one lost

his sons in a terrible war and the second lost all his money
and died considerably poorer than he was born.*

Of course, each of the husband's new mates suffered just
by living with these men. And perhaps this was a more
severe punishment than they deserved.

The wise cat struggled to provide for her large family for
many years. It was not an easy life but she became even
more wise and learned to tell the difference between good
people and wicked ones. It was only a matter of time before
a truly fine husband would appear to change her life. But
the wise cat was in no hurry to find another husband. She
did not forget that the world is full of greedy, stupid and
dishonourable people. She had learned to rely on her own
strength. Although this solitary way of life was perilous,
the cat preferred living by her wits to living with a fool.
She was content knowing that she didn't have a husband
who could cheat or abandon her. However, good fortune
brought her face to face with a perfect match, one who was
her equal in wisdom and strength with no trace of greed
or foolishness.

She was a wise cat of course and knew not to jump at
any prospect of marriage. She had learned the wisdom
of investigating any risky situation. The perfect match
was clearly available, and interested in caring for her and
taking over the protection of her little ones, but the wise
cat feigned indifference and waited. This was a wise tactic,
because things which appear to be perfect often have a
rotten core. When no sign of rottenness showed itself,
when no word of hidden things reached her, the wise cat
put her protests aside. She knew the time was right to

---

* This is a particularly crucial comment with regard to Oum Mohammed's
life story. Although she does not mention the death of her first husband's sons
in her own story, it is common knowledge among local women. These young
men were killed in the Arab-Israeli wars. Several friends and neighbours
commented on the natural justice of this tragedy, remembering that Oum
Mohammed was divorced for failing to bear her first husband sons.

change her mind, otherwise the perfect match might grow accustomed to her refusals, take her apparent lack of interest at face value and stop asking to marry her. One day, right out of the blue, the wise cat shocked the would-be husband by giving in to his greatest desire and agreeing to be his wife. She was not cautious or coy about this. That is not the style of a cat destined to be old and wise.

From this experience the cat learned that there is nothing to be gained by timidity and false modesty. She never forgot that good timing is a useful skill. In every battle the triumphant side chooses when and where and how to launch its attack.

The wise cat and her new husband settled down to a fine life. Many more kittens swelled the numbers of their already large family. They were not wealthy but were comfortable and happy. The cat had found happiness and contentment but was wise enough not to take them for granted. Free from the burden of hunting for food, she was able to devote herself to her kittens and she brought them up with a fair and firm hand. At last her life seemed free from hardship. But the unexpected has a curious way of creeping into our life and changing things.

What was to happen to the wise cat now, surely she was not to be abandoned by her perfect match? Of course not!

This time pain was to reappear in the wise cat's life, not heartbreaking pain but physical pain which burned and stabbed her limbs. It was not an expected source of pain! The pain which troubled the wise cat was linked to her troubled past. But never mind the actual source of the pain, this is unimportant. Let's just say that it was linked to the wise cat's past and leave it at that!*

The wise cat suffered greatly with each new attack of

---

* The teller spoke with notable vehemence at this point in the narrative as if keen to move on, regretting her reference to the cause of the cat's pain. In her life story Oum Mohammed speaks of the pain she suffers with complete conviction that it is caused by a curse worked by Nadia, the woman her second husband married. It is interesting to note that Oum Mohammed will not

pain. She tried to find a cure, but without success, so she learned to live with the pain. The important thing is that her wisdom saved her again and she learned to think of the pain as a reminder of past hardship in relation to her happy present. The wise cat learned that you can never be complacent or confident of a happy future because there is always something which crops up unexpectedly to cloud the horizon. She never forgot that determination is a better source of strength than pride. Of course the wise cat was proud of her many triumphs, but experience had taught her that pride is a dangerous emotion if it is not kept in check.

During the years to come the wise cat grew even wiser and the creatures which had once admired her from afar came to know her wisdom from personal experience. As the wise cat grew older the demands on her time and energy lessened as her family left home to make their own way in the world. But the wise old cat did not waste her free time on selfish pleasure. A generous nature prompted the wise old cat to encourage other creatures to look to her for advice. Each day she sat on her fine cushion and received a constant stream of visitors who hoped for a few wise words to make sense of their problems.

All who approached the wise old cat went away feeling that they could find a way of coping with whatever hardship they had to face. They all were inspired by the example of the wise old cat whose triumphant spirit gave everyone a sense that they could themselves triumph over disaster. The wise old cat was generous and hospitable, and most important of all, she dared to speak her mind. Confronted with foolishness, greed, timidity or pride, she was not afraid to point out a weakness or to suggest a harsh remedy which would be unpopular.

A scraggy dog once ventured to the wise cat's home. This was quite an unusual and unexpected event. For one

---

tolerate mention of Nadia among her friends, fearing that this will intensify the force of the curse.

thing it is a brave act to search for advice in any quarter and this was a very timid dog. Moreover, dogs and cats are not often on friendly terms, quite the opposite in fact. For another thing, this dog was known to be so timid that it was considered a lost cause, too scared to try to face up to the troubles it seemed to attract.

The wise old cat welcomed the dog and immediately praised its decision to come to see her. The dog hung its head and told her that everything was hopeless. The wise old cat laughed, but not unkindly. She had lived through many hard times and had learned a lot about feelings of hope and despair. She said: 'Forget hope! One thing I have learned in my long life is that it's better to struggle and fight. First things first, decide to deal with your problems, do something about them and when you see the results, then hope will follow by itself.'

The timid dog had expected the wise old cat to scold it for failing to be brave. Instead the cat had spoken kindly and firmly, which gave the dog courage. The cat was too wise to do the expected thing all the time. The timid dog was so surprised at these words that it forgot to be timid! The dog stared at the cat and announced: 'You're right! I have decided to face up to my problems and do something about them. I'll start immediately!' The cat gave a contented smile and the dog was overcome with gratitude. It thanked the wise old cat and set off more determined than before, with its head held high.

Once a fine-looking rooster strutted up to the cat's home. He was clearly a very proud bird and thought highly of himself. The wise old cat noticed this and guessed what the rooster's problem was. The proud rooster was nervous and anxious. He was keen to pretend that this was just a social call and acted the part of an important guest. First the rooster strutted and preened. Then it talked about the weather and politics and local news. Finally the cat interrupted and regarded the rooster with displeasure: 'Do you have a problem or not? Perhaps you're here by mistake. This isn't a coffee house you know.' The wise old cat assumed a determined tone to shame the proud rooster: 'I don't engage in idle chatter, I try to advise those who choose to ask me!' These were harsh words, but the wise old cat always adopted the attitude which best suited her visitors.

The rooster finally confessed his problem. He was growing old and was afraid of losing his fine looks. What was worse, he was sure that his wives were making fun of him, he couldn't make them behave, they ignored his commands and did whatever they liked!

The rooster worked himself into a fury as he revealed his worries. The wise old cat let him rave and make even more of a fool of himself, then started to smile. Suddenly the rooster noticed and stopped in mid-sentence. He puffed out his chest and demanded: 'Are you laughing at me too? I did not come to here to be insulted by an old cat! What an outrage!'

The smile disappeared from the cat's face in an instant. She turned on the proud rooster and stared at him until he looked away in fear. 'I know all about your problems,' she said. 'I know their solution too. Do you want to hear or not?' she asked. The rooster nodded, since he was too tongue-tied and didn't dare to speak. 'I have three things to say. Listen hard!' the cat warned. 'First, you're an old rooster so act your age. Second, don't be so proud and pretend that you're still king of the hen house. Third, discuss things with your wives, talk to them sensibly and don't make stupid demands.' The wise cat paused to let this sink in and then continued: 'Don't forget they've lived with your proud ways for many years, old rooster. I don't think it's surprising that your wives misbehave if you're always making such a fool of yourself!'

The rooster had never been spoken to like this before. He had expected sympathy and advice on how to punish his wives, not abuse and criticism. But the wise old cat always knew when it was best to be tough. The rooster would not have listened to her advice if she had treated him with respect, that would have swelled his pride further and increased his stupidity. When the rooster departed he was a little more humble and a much nicer creature.

The timid dog and the proud rooster were only two of the creatures who were privileged to hear the old cat's words of wisdom. This would become a tale of one thousand and one nights if it described just half the creatures who had come to sit by the cushion of the wise old cat. Of course the wise old cat is still there sitting on her fine cushion, dispensing wise words and sharing her wit and wisdom with anyone who visits. Anyone who knows the wise old cat loves and respects her, and *everyone* knows her! It is not easy for them to find words to express the gratitude and admiration they feel because, of course, they are not as wise or clever as she. But they know that she knows this, after all, she is the wise old cat who knows everything!

After the tale's closing sentence there was an immediate enthusiastic chorus of 'How true!', 'Yes indeed!' and 'Too right!'. Given Oum Mohammed's local prestige and social position, this was one occasion when there was no attempt to tell a tale with masked references or subtle meanings. Indeed the tale of the Wise Old Cat is less of a tale than an eulogy to Oum Mohammed. However, this increased rather than diminished the impact of the tale.

The tale had its desired effect on both Oum Mohammed and the company of women. The storyteller had gauged the required tone from a certainty that everyone wanted their admiration for Oum Mohammed to be given a voice. There was no doubt that she had found the perfect vehicle for the company's strong sentiments. The grand old woman sat on her stool and grinned. I thought that Oum Mohammed had never appeared more impressive and regal. Her already colossal body seemed to expand with every flattering comment, and she looked like a sleek glowing Buddah in the dim light. Oum Mohammed's delight was unmistakable, indeed it was marked by an unusual silence. She even renounced the role of bountiful hostess and asked Amira to serve the final round of cakes. For once, being the absolute prima donna, Oum Mohammed was overcome by what only can be called a state of speechless glee.

LAILA: A REBELLIOUS WOMAN

Laila is a young woman who lives in the same street as Oum Mohammed, but her view of women's lives could not be more different. When I recorded Laila's life story I soon realised that she was more interested in exploring ideas and expectations about the future than describing her personal experience of growing up in the city. Laila sees the problems of older women through the rebellious eyes of youth. She spent a lot of time with me during fieldwork, helping me to collect genealogial data and marriage records in the neighbourhood and discussing her own ideals and aspirations with great enthusiasm. Her sharp critical comments on women's place in society set her apart from the older generation of women. Although she lives within this community, her future experiences are unlikely to match her dreams in full; her ideas place her firmly within an emergent new generation of women who may come to look for personal fulfilment beyond the horizon of marriage and family.

I'm not as old or wise as many of the other women, but that's not to say that I've no experience of the world or that I've no ideas of my own. I may be just seventeen but the important thing is that my whole life is ahead of me, and I mean to make the best of every chance I have. I am the third daughter of a family of seven and I was the last daughter born before the four sons who are my parents' pride and joy. I don't imagine that there was a great celebration at my birth, after three girls in a row my mother must have feared that she would never have a son!

My brothers are a big source of annoyance to me. What makes it worse than usual (since sisters always have lots of complaints about their younger brothers) is that there are four of them and they're terribly spoiled. They always get their own way, they only have to ask for something and it appears before them as if by magic, whereas if I want something, even some necessity like new shoes, my mother acts as if I'm asking for the moon.

There are times when I think my mother is really stupid, God forgive me for saying it, but it's how I feel. For instance, she can't see how my brothers manipulate her with all their tricks. They are never grateful or polite to her, no matter what she does for them. They even make fun of her behind her back, calling her the old crone and so on. I've heard them with my own ears, but of course she'd never believe me if I told her and she'd put it down to my jealousy. That's one of her favourite sayings: you're only jealous of your brothers, Laila, grow up and behave like a woman. Like a grown woman she says! It's clear to me that her idea of a grown woman is one who is at the beck and call of every man in the world. The big problem for women around here like my mother is that they never have time to think of their own welfare.

I know my mother would accuse me of having modern ideas if she heard me say this, but I don't care. I don't care if people say I'm rebellious. I don't see what's so wrong with trying to stand up for yourself. People never say that it's a bad thing when boys defend themselves. If my mother had more sense she would have a happier life and my brothers would be nicer young men. There are four of them, aged from nine to fifteen, and I think that they grow worse the older they get. The oldest of them, Ali, the one born after me, is really horrible and he encourages the younger ones to imitate him. There must be some nice men in the world but they are probably the ones who had no older brothers to teach them how to treat women badly.

When boys start going off with their fathers to spend time in the coffee house and then work alongside their fathers and the other men, I think that's when they realise that the women at home are different. In their eyes women are just there to cook and clean and they begin to think that they're special because they're out in the world. I'm sure that the men all feed each other stories of their own importance outside the house, then they treat their sisters and mothers like dirt when they come home. If I ever have a son I'm going to keep him out of male company as much as possible. I'll make sure that he appreciates all the work women do at home and I'll teach him to be kind and gentle to his sisters.

It's true that a woman's sons are very useful when she grows old and needs their support. That's one reason why every mother makes a big fuss about her sons, but there must be other people who can provide this help in your old age. Look at the women around here, they're always helping each other out and of course their husbands usually do nothing. The husbands never notice this and behave as if their food cooks itself. Maybe if women could dare to admit this they'd see that men are not much use at all. And that's another terrible thing I've said, even if it's true!

Young women might be able to think like this more often if their mothers didn't fill their heads with so much nonsense. There's nothing for girls to listen to apart from talk about being proper and modest and looking forward to marriage. There's nothing wrong with being a wife of course, I'm not that stupid or rebellious, but I think that it would be nice if you could be a different kind of wife. I mean, things change and why live the same kind of life as your own mother did?

The television is always showing you that people do things differently in different places, so why not here? Money makes a big difference of course and perhaps the men would be nicer to us if we were all well off. I think that women who have money are lucky because they can buy whatever they want and they don't have to depend on anyone. If you're rich and your father is really cross, then you can go off and look after yourself and you don't have to pretend to be sorry and ashamed just because he's the boss. My friends have this problem all the time, but they're stuck in a situation where they have to follow their father's every command, even when it's completely stupid. I think it's crazy! Parents will always disagree with their children but there has to be a better way to deal with disagreements than beating people into submission.

My father died six years ago. I was just a child then and I have no strong feelings about it. At the time I only was aware that something sad had happened. I remember when people said that my father was dead I burst into tears, but I don't think that I really understood what they were saying. I never knew my father well, I mean that he seemed like a stranger in the house. Maybe it's because I was very young then, but I have no memories of him playing with me or paying any attention to me. Now I can hardly remember what he looked like.

There is one photograph of him in the living room but it shows him as a very young man on his wedding day. In the picture he has very dark hair and is smiling, but his hair was grey when I was a child and I didn't see him smile very often. My mother looks very beautiful in the picture. She is beside my father, smiling at him and wearing a lovely dress. She looks like a princess or a great lady from a rich family. When you look at her now it's hard to think that she's the woman in that old photograph. I know that his death ruined her. I'm not exaggerating, she became an old woman overnight as if the fact that she was a widow had aged her twenty years in less than one day.

My mother never stops worrying about money. Money for Ali's school books, money for Karim's new shoes and so on. This is the song she sings all the time and it's always about the boys and their needs. She's never concerned about my sisters or me. We have to worry about ourselves since my brothers use up all her energy. My mother started to work full time after my father's death and as soon as my sisters and I were old enough we had to join her. We act like slaves in order to earn money to feed my greedy brothers.

The world is upside-down in our house because the boys are at home while their womenfolk are out in the carpet workshop. We work ourselves to exhaustion every day to put food on the table.

I've been a slave in that workshop since I was about twelve. There was almost no time for school and I was never allowed to study at home, although I'm much cleverer than my brothers. I even help them with their school work now. I don't do their lessons for them because they demand it or to make school easier for them, in fact I hope they all fail their exams and that would show them that I'm clever and they're the stupid ones. I only agree to help them because I really enjoy it and I like thinking about things and working things out. I love deciding how to answer questions in subjects like history and literature. Television is a good way to get to know about things for people who can't get to school. I love television and watch it whenever I can in order to learn things. Television means that I can educate myself even if I'm not able to read very much and I'm not properly educated because I had just a few years at school. If I was granted one magic wish it would be to go back to school. I think that I would even choose this before wishing for the best husband in the world!

The question of a husband is a huge problem for me. It's not just because of all the things I've said about men not being nice, but also because our family is not well off and marriages cost a lot of money. My mother is always threatening me by saying that no one will ever marry me. She says that no man would want me for a wife because I'm too quarrelsome. This is her biggest threat, it's the worst thing she can think of, and believe me, she has lots of terrible threats. But my mother's real problem is money, it's got nothing to do with what she says about me being nasty and bossy. Despite all her threats, I know she doesn't really believe this.

If she gets her way, I'll end up being married to a poor man from the next street. Her plan is to marry me to the first idiot who seems interested and I know that she'll accept any offer like a shot. The same goes for my sisters; my mother will be happy when my sisters and I are all poor wives with poor husbands. If that happens we'll go on making carpets in the workshop forever. What a disaster!

I hope none of this happens and I have my own ideas about how to cope with my mother's plans for my marriage when the time comes. My sisters think I'm a bit crazy and maybe they're right, but I still think I'm smarter than they are. For instance, I see how they're starting to get silly about the prospect of a wedding. They start putting on airs and acting high and mighty when they meet any man who might turn out to be a candidate for marriage. Life is very difficult for them because they're so desperate to get married. I suppose I'm better off than them because I'm the youngest daughter and I'm not in a hurry to find a man. If you're still single at twenty like my oldest sister, it's something to worry about because people start to say that there's something wrong with you.

There is talk that both my sisters will be engaged before Ramadan and I know the two idiots who are the likely candidates. My mother has been trying to arrange things with these men's families. It's been her main concern for more than a month now and this is a sign that the deal is going well. She's always fussing about cakes and tea parties for our potential in-laws in order to make a good impression. This is another of her favourite phrases at present. These days she never stops telling me to make a good impression: to fix my hair and make a good impression, to keep my mouth shut and make a good impression, to act like a nice shy little girl and make a good impression. It's hell! I try to behave properly at these tea parties for my sisters' sakes, and while I'm not very good at it, at least I don't cause complete chaos. These men and their families don't think much of me but that's fine, it doesn't matter since I'm not the one they want to marry.

How I behave and what people think is an important

part of the plan that I mentioned earlier. It's very simple. At the moment I'm prepared to make a good impression in the hope that my sisters will be considered respectable enough to marry, but it'll be quite different when it comes to the build-up to my own engagement. I think it won't be too hard to destroy my chances of marriage by reverting to my usual bad behaviour. After all, no man wants a rebellious wife, isn't that what my mother is always saying? When the time comes I'll simply apply her rule to my own ends. I can just imagine her face when she sees how I behave when she invites some awful would-be husband and his family to the house. 'Watch your manners and make a good impression,' she'll say, and of course I'll do my best to be as rude and undesirable as possible.

Of course if my plan works and I manage to scare off would-be husbands, will I be worse off? I don't know anyone who doesn't have a husband and of course it's unthinkable never to have married. My mother would be incredibly angry if she had any idea that I'm not very keen on getting married. If she knew about my plan she'd probably throw me out of the house and leave me to look after myself. This would be a nightmare. It would be such a shameful situation and people would say all sorts of awful things about me. I think I would have to go away from this area to live somewhere where people didn't know me. But there must be a lot of single women looking after themselves in the world so it can't be impossible. It's just a very frightening idea for me because nobody around here could cope with it. Nobody knows how to look after themselves, at least the women don't, that's what I'm saying, but I don't think that there is any reason why people can't change and learn new things.

What I really want is a way of life that is quite different from my mother's. People are always criticising the new ways of the city which are different from the old ones, but things are just changing, that's all. I don't see what can be so bad about that. People want new clothes and new houses and things like this all the time, so why don't they like new ideas? The old people talk about the countryside as if it was straight out of a wonderful, exciting film. I can't believe the countryside is really that wonderful; if it was why did everybody leave and come to the city? Some old women are as bad as the men when they go on about country life. They tell you about the countrywomen in the old days who all lived in a kind of paradise. They were proud, happy, hard-working and free from drudgery, unlike modern women in the cities. But if you ask them why things were like this, they can't explain it. If you ask them again, they just get cross and talk about ignorant young people who don't know about the good old days and country values.

I don't think that any of this makes sense. Why can't things get better in the city? Life isn't perfect here, but I suspect that the good old days weren't much better. I think that women would be able to forget the past and start to improve their families' lives in the city if they weren't so worn out by their husbands' stupid dreams and selfish troubles. That's the real problem, women always have to make everybody feel better and pretend that they've no troubles of their own. First, you have to make sure that your father is happy, then you must keep your brothers and uncles and all the men of the family happy, then finally when you marry, you have to spend all your time being cheerful in order to make your husband happy. It seems very unfair to me. What a waste of energy! I think it's unfair and a waste of a woman's energy because there is nobody to worry about her own happiness.

I think I'd be very happy if I was able to look after myself, just me and and nobody else. Think of widows. Now they're a good example of women who look after their own needs and provide for themselves. Nobody criticises widows, it's quite the opposite in fact. After the sympathy for their sad plight, everyone remarks how well Widow So-and-so is coping, how successful she's become, how much she's learned about trade or whatever. I'd like people to say things like that about me. If I manage to avoid the idiots my mother will try to get me to marry, I might even find a nice husband when I'm a bit older and have more ideas about the world. And once my brothers are older, they'll have to start earning money for themselves and then I'll be able to save all the spare cash I can.

I often wonder about what's going to happen to me in the future. I worry about having all these ideas and I wouldn't dare to mention them to anyone else here. My mother is right when she calls me a big bag of trouble. Maybe I'll wake up some day soon and find that I don't feel rebellious any more, that would make life a lot easier for everybody. Or better still, maybe I'll find someone who is just as rebellious as I am and we'll run away together!

Right now I'd prefer to forget about marriage and go on working. First of all, I want to find a better job, one which really interests me. If I had a good job with a higher wage it would mean that I could buy things for myself with my own money. There are all sorts of jobs which women can do in the modern world, that's what is so good about city life, you have more options than in the countryside. I wouldn't want to spend all day chasing goats or planting crops. It would be great to have a job which made you use your brains. I would be happy earning money for myself in some interesting way, it would be a new kind of life for a woman. One day when I'm older I'd like to have a stall of my own like the widows in the market and sell things. Wouldn't it be wonderful if you could be a widow without getting married first!

Laila succeeded in driving off all the suitors her mother invited to tea during the time I spent in the neighbourhood. Shortly before I left, she convinced the workshop manager that she could look after orders and deliveries and gave up her menial job to work in the general office. She vehemently denied having any romantic interest in the workshop's new, highly skilled weaver, describing their relationship as 'properly businesslike', but admited that in principle he is the sort of man she would not object to marrying one day. After her fiery words, perhaps we should not be surprised that thus far Laila's ambitions are unchecked and that her dream of a new kind of life remains intact.

OUM ALI: A PESSIMISTIC WOMAN

Whenever the women meet, Oum Ali seems to be everywhere at once, on the fringes of all conversations. She has a ready supply of self-centred comments to add to any gossip as long as it concerns some misfortune or tragedy. She usually sits with Amira and Oum Karim and relies on their sympathetic responses to back up her own catalogue of woe. When a tale is told Oum Ali's preoccupation with disaster shines through in the tragic episodes. She excels in contributing little squeals and gasps at key moments of suspense, punctuated with cries of 'How dreadful!' A sharp nudge from one of the other women, usually Oum Idris, is the only thing which prevents Oum Ali from interrupting the storyteller, no doubt to remark that her own experiences are more tragic than those described in a mere tale. This impression of Oum Ali seems unfair when her problems are taken into consideration. This is how she views the events which have dominated her life.

The story of my life will shock you when you hear about the terrible things I have had to bear. How I have survived to talk about it surprises even me. I was born into a good family, a well off family in a village in the south of the Delta area. I had a perfect childhood, perfect in every way, like my mother and her mother and all the women of their family lines. Women lived like princesses in my father's family, they did not have to work or worry or bother themselves with things that did not concern them. They ruled over the home while the men took care of the outside world. There was no question of them having to deal with money matters or with scraping together funds for food or bills. That is how things should be, of course, although in a place like this you might forget it.

My father was from a proud line. His people had good land and the skill to work it. But I was still a child when the first disaster of my life struck. My father was cheated out of a section of his most fertile land by a long-time enemy of his family. This meant that we were suddenly poor. After the hard work of all his ancestors my father was suddenly no better than a landless peasant. We, the women of the household, cried for weeks while my father and his brothers tried to get the land back, but it was hopeless. The family who had stolen our land had important allies in powerful places and they were able to overrule every objection my father raised. A sudden change of fortune, that is the thing from long ago that I remember most clearly, and that change of fortune pointed out the direction my life was to take. Things had started off well, but when my childhood was near an end they started to get worse and worse.

Just look at me now! Can you look at me and imagine that I once was a sweet child raised in luxury, protected from all harm and adored by everyone!

My wonderful father was destroyed by the loss of his land. Although he had not lost everything, the sections of land which remained his had poor soil and were far from the house. We suddenly knew what hunger was for the first time. My older sisters had been married by then and I was the last girl without a husband. Of course with the change in fortune I was destined for a poor marriage, unlike my proud sisters whose husbands came from other fine families. They all escaped the disaster caused by the down-turn in my father's fortune. They all were safe in the protection of their husbands' prosperous families.

My parents did the best they could when they arranged my marriage, but naturally it wasn't ideal or even adequate. They found me a husband from a family who had also suffered at the hands of this predatory land-grabbing lot. But since this had happened some years earlier my husband was not brought up as a gentleman but as a peasant. He was used to the sight of his mother and sisters toiling in the field with the menfolk, not sitting at home in the shade sewing and chatting and devoting themselves to their children. He was not a bad man, let me make that clear, but he was not my equal. He had no experience of the fine things in life and no expectations that they might come within his reach.

I feel that my marriage was arranged and my fate sealed before I noticed. A speedy marriage was essential from my father's point of view, his last unmarried daughter had to be taken care of before he died. Indeed, I think he felt his life was coming to an end because he had lost his land. My wedding feast was not as splendid as my sisters' feasts and I was upset by this. I still am when I think of it all these years later! I wept when I saw how plain my dress was, it was a terrible poor girl's wedding dress! Of course my bridal gifts and jewellery also were a mere fraction of what my sisters had received. I wept until my eyes were all puffy and my wedding day was ruined. Of course the worse was yet to come although I did not know it at the time.

During the wedding feast my new husband announced that we were to go to the city. What a nightmare! All the guests cheered and wished us luck. What a joke! If they had thrown stones I would not have been more horrified. The decision to move had nothing to do with me, it wasn't up to me to choose and I had no right to question my new husband. I was helpless and could raise no objection. What a terrible wedding day! Of course from that day on I was part of my husband's family. I was in his care and under his protection. His protection! That would be a joke if it wasn't a tragedy!

Everyone in the village gathered to wave when we set off for the city. It was considered to be a very brave thing to do, or perhaps it was more like a last resort for people with no other option. Bravery and courage were qualities I never noticed in my husband's case! We had to walk most of the way to the city and I was soon weeping with anger against fate. My feet bled and my new shoes were destroyed by the miles of rough ground we had to cross. Naturally I had expected that we would catch a bus to the city, but my husband said it was better to go on foot. He had so little hope for the future that he wanted us to save money from the outset. He said that the money we saved by not paying bus fares would give us some extra security until we established ourselves in the city. But I was persistent in my complaints and he finally gave in to my tears. We travelled the last twenty miles by bus. However, when I saw the city for the first time I wished we had walked the whole way since that would have delayed our arrival.

To my eyes the city was worse than a desert. It was just as ugly and barren, but crammed with people. Everywhere you looked there were crowds of poor people who were dirty, ill-mannered and ill-dressed. Everyone shouted and yelled at each other, there was no politeness and no sign of modest behaviour. It seemed that people in the city had become animals! The women were out in the streets yelling as loud as the men and were even selling things. I was astonished to see that women were working alongside men, since I had always thought that city people were prosperous and refined. This might sound curious coming from me now, but however cruel fate has been, I will never forget that I was born to a different life.

The first months in the city were a worse nightmare than the first sight of it. Of course my husband had no useful contacts. The people he knew in the neighbourhood were as destitute as we were, the city had offered them no chances. So much for the better life he was going to make for us! We spent the first year living in a tiny rough room he built alongside his friend's dwelling. I tried to keep it clean but there wasn't much I could do with it. I had a few bits of furniture and a bed roll, a fine state of affairs for a new bride. My husband, God rest his soul, searched for work day and night. But he could only manage to find a collection of ill-paid, poor people's jobs which left him exhausted or depressed. This was my earliest experience of despair. Still, I should say that my husband tried his best and he was very happy when I became pregnant, but his best was not good enough. He was not my equal and did not have the stamina and brains which are bred into fine families.

I felt worn out with the dirt and noise of the city throughout my pregnancy. In the end the child I had carried only lived for a few hours.

God forgive me if I sin by saying this, but I feel that this son of mine took one look at the world he had been born into and chose a quick escape. My husband was distressed, but of course he didn't accept that he was the real cause of the disaster. He didn't have enough experience of caring for women to know that a woman in a delicate condition should be protected from all strain, particularly when hardship and toil are new to her. But an easy life was not my fate. My husband and I grew more distant after the baby's death. It was not a happy marriage. He continued to earn a few pennies in his assortment of odd jobs, I continued to struggle to make ends meet.

Naturally I saw that other women in the neighbourhood were working, but I didn't take a job myself. What could I have done in those days? I didn't know that women don't need to have a particular skill to get a job. Certainly, in those days it didn't occur to me that things would never improve! When I was pregnant for the second time my husband tried to take more care of me. A daughter was born after this difficult pregnancy and my suffering was a sign that she would be a difficult child. Since the day of her birth she has been nothing but trouble. She can't manage the smallest task without creating more work through her stupidity and forgetfulness. She is no help at all to her poor widowed mother.

After my daughter was born things got worse and worse. Times were as hard as they had ever been and I had to find a job. I finally started to work with the leather dealer, stitching and binding leather strips until my fingers were raw. I loathed this work and I still do, although in those days I had a faint hope that I wouldn't have to work for long. It's curious but I can hardly remember getting this job, I slipped into work without realising it. A neighbour arranged things with the dealer, his boy delivered the leather and gave me instructions, I did the sewing and binding, then my first wages came. It was as simple as that. Suddenly I was a working woman, the very thing I had despised most about life among the poor of the city.

Around that time I had another son, a fat healthy baby who seemed to thrive on what poor milk I could give him until, of course, fate played another cruel trick. My baby weakened, almost overnight, and he died before he was three months old. It may seem as if I'm hard and heartless because I can talk about all these disasters without any sign of grief, but there has been so much grief in my life that my heart can't feel anything except fear. I live in terror of the next disaster and know it will be worse than the last.

After my second son died my husband started to weaken too, although I didn't really notice this at the time. I became pregnant again and had another son. This time the baby didn't die, but I am terrified by the thought of his death. What a cruel fate to have given birth to two fine boys who die, then to have a tiny, sickly son who just manages to survive. I can hardly believe that my boy Ali has reached the age of six, although he is not out of danger yet and I feel that he may die at any time. He has never been well and is a very weak child. Poor little Ali is always in need of medicine and constant care.* If I was rich I would take him to the best doctors who might be able to cure him, but as it is, I struggle to find the money to pay for drugs from

---

* Ali had no serious illness during the time I spent in the neighbourhood. The local view of his state of heath was that Oum Ali was over-protective of her son and tended to upgrade a cough to pneumonia. This criticism of Oum Ali, remembering the fact that local mothers are more protective of their sons than is common in western society, implies that her concern about his chance of survival is exaggerated. Oum Ali spends a considerable portion of her meagre earnings on pharmacy bills, which suggests that her fears about Ali's health, however unfounded, are genuine.

the pharmacist. These things keep him alive and he gets the best food I can afford, although my daughter and I go hungry as a result.

My husband died just after Ali was born and it makes me sad to think that Sherif died before he knew that he had a son who might reach manhood. My husband died as quietly as he had lived. It was like he just melted away under the pressures of life. I have not mentioned the fact that Sherif's death was a great blow, but indeed it was. Remember that I was alone in the city without family or many friends. Local people were kind and full of sympathy of course, but pity won't fill empty stomachs. There was no alternative but to accept that I had to be both father and mother to my children. I had to earn the money to feed them, and at the same time keep a tidy house and provide them with a mother's care. I was starting to learn that the future is an unknown land full of more dangers than you can imagine.

Since that time I have tried to do my best although I've been burdened down with worries and fear of the future. I have some good friends now who help out with small things whenever they can. We work for the same trader and have to put up with his petty demands, discourtesies and injustices. We often work together in the same room since these women have their youngsters to look after too. I suppose that I could take a job away from home like other women, but I refuse to. I think that I'd rather die of starvation than work in the streets like a man. That would be a total rejection of my past way of life, even though those days of my childhood are no more than a distant memory. But I earn just enough to make ends meet by working at home, and my daughter Fatima will start work as soon as possible in order to save something for her marriage.

It will be an enormous relief when Fatima is old enough to get married. A husband will take her off my hands, if I can find some sort of decent man for her. The problem is that she doesn't have many virtues or charms which I can advertise. She certainly isn't pretty, because she didn't inherit my features, and I'm particularly worried about her clumsiness.* Of course I'll find a man for her in the end, even the most foolish and useless girls manage to get a husband. But I'm worried that it will take longer than usual and there's also the question of money. There is always the question of money! Unless she changes her ways she won't have much to offer a prospective husband. Perhaps I can get her a job in one of the local workshops. I don't approve of young girls working away from home, but the wages are better and she won't be the only girl from the neighbourhood earning her dowry there.

I am never free from worry about Ali. He is my pride and joy, although he is so weak. I have great plans for him and sometimes I dare to think that he might save us all in the end. If he survives he could become an important man and get an office job. Then he would earn the kind of money which would change our whole way of life. I am sad when I think about the childhood he would have had if we lived in a village. He would grow into a strong man with the fresh air and healthy farm work. The life of a farmer isn't easy of course, it's hard work and not all of it is pleasant because the land is a hard master. But the countryside produces good strong people. I think it's because of the clean air and healthy way of life. There is also a special kind of strength which develops in a man who works for his family on his own soil. This brings out the best in a man, though it didn't quite reach my own husband, God rest his soul!

Perhaps we will find a way to return to the country some

---

* Clumsiness is considered a serious fault in a girl. A traditional test of dexterity involves shelling a hot egg. A bride will often have to perform this task in front of her prospective mother-in-law and female in-laws. It is important that the egg-white is unscarred and the flesh is unmarked. Oum Ali's daughter Fatima did not seem any more clumsy than a normal eight year old. However, Oum Ali's constant criticism and Fatima's awareness of her mother's low expectations made her nervous and she often dropped things and made mistakes performing chores under supervision.

day. When Ali grows up and gets married we could go back home and turn his wife into a good rural woman. I have worked out exactly what sort of woman Ali needs. She must be clever and hard-working and show all the signs of being a strong mother. Whatever difficulties present themselves or whatever hardship is involved, and of course nothing is ever easy, I will find him this kind of wife if there is a good enough girl in the city. It would be best of all to have enough money to travel back to my home village and find Ali a wife from my father's kin and allies. Village girls always make better brides, they are stronger and better looking, but everything comes down to money in the end and it isn't likely that I could afford to arrange his marriage to a bride from outside the city.

But all this talk of the future is dangerous and I should not tempt fate by it. I must only think of tomorrow and not too far ahead in case Ali falls ill and dies, God forbid! I must concentrate all my efforts on making sure that he reaches manhood and is strong enough to be a good husband and father.

If I can dare to dream a little about the future I see myself back in the village of my childhood. My son has a family of his own and I am surrounded by grandchildren and cousins and the rest of my kin. I will sit in the shade of a tree and watch the world go by, secure in the knowledge that Ali will take good care of me in my old age. I can remember the happy times from my own childhood when I hadn't a care in the world and I didn't know what fear or sorrow was. I was such a happy little girl who lived in ignorance and innocence of how her life was to change under fate's cruel hand. How different my life used to be! Once I was free from fear and want, now I live in a trap just waiting for the next disaster to happen.

If I ever see my home village again and die a countrywoman it will be the only good thing that has happened in my adult life. Surely I deserve one final reward for all the hard times and suffering I have experienced in the city?

But I suppose that things have changed in all villages. I can imagine that a great many things are different in my old village these days. The people will not be the same and the place itself will be unrecognisable. So even if I escaped from this terrible city, no doubt I would find myself in an even worse situation.

One evening the following tale forced Oum Ali to cut short what Oum Idris calls 'another report from the war zone'.

THE FOOLISH BEETLE

This is a tale about the foolishness of some creatures. Creatures like this may have troubles, but their foolishness comes from treating small fears like big ones.

Once there was a huge forest which teemed with all kinds of life. It was not a beautiful forest, but it was not ugly. It was not a safe place, neither a dangerous one. It was just a forest and like most forests it had its nice spots and its less pleasant ones. Some of the creatures who lived there liked the forest a lot and would never dream of leaving it. Others were too busy searching for food and looking out for themselves to have much of an opinion of their habitation. However, there was one creature which never thought about anything else: that was the foolish beetle.

This beetle was not a bad creature, just foolish. It spent the day running in circles through the undergrowth. It covered a lot of ground but with no clear purpose. It went up and down over mounds of grass, across streams, under fallen tree trunks, then around and around in circles again. Usually it was worn out by afternoon and would sink under a leaf to sleep for a while before starting off on another foolish run. The beetle spent every day in the same foolish way. It wasted energy and time and achieved nothing. It never noticed the juicy leaves and tasty morsels which lay in its path but ran straight past them. Sometimes the beetle even tripped over a grub, the perfect dinner, and still didn't notice. 'Damn damn damn!' it would mutter angrily. 'What bad luck! Why do I have the misfortune to be tripped up by things when I've so much to do!'

The toads sat on their lily pads and watched the beetle. Sometimes they felt sorry for the beetle, but mostly they were fed up with the way it was always complaining about things. The toads liked the forest and were content with the life it offered them. They were fat and prone to laziness, but they always finished whatever tasks they set themselves without complaint or unnecessary fuss. In fact the toads had a great number of dangers to face in their search for food. There were all sorts of dangers outside the forest. Every evening they hopped away from their watery home towards the outside world. They did not travel far, but once they reached the place where people lived they did not hesitate. The toads would leap inside these strange mud-brick shells and feast on fat mosquitoes. The huge creatures who lived in the houses tried to crush them with brooms and spear them with sticks.* Even the lazy toads overcame their fears for the sake of their little ones back at the pond.

The family of honey bees rarely had a minute of free time, but they would catch an occasional glimpse of the foolish beetle. Day after day they watched it in amusement or disapproval. Down below in the undergrowth the beetle was always chasing some enemy or searching for some tasty meal in a pointless fashion, convinced that it was going in the right direction. Everything the beetle did was disorganised because the foolish beetle imagined things that did not exist, especially insuperable problems and omens of misfortune. The beetle and its family were often

---

* Toads are a common sight in most Egyptian villages, especially in the Delta area. At dusk they leave the canals and irrigation ditches in the pursuit of mosquitoes and flies. It is not unusual to see a toad chasing insects across the floor of a hut, bounding in through a window or leaping up a wall. Children look forward to these sudden appearances and 'toad chasing' is a popular evening entertainment for local boys.

hungry because all its efforts came to nothing. Sometimes the bees felt sorry for the foolish beetle and tried to bring its attention to the food which was under its nose. But most of their efforts were in vain. 'It might hear us if it didn't complain so much,' said one bee. But the beetle was only interested in listening to itself.

The foolish beetle had a little song it liked to sing while it ran around in circles. The song went like this:

> *Poor little me, all alone*
> *Life is hard so far from home*
> *Life is sad and so unfair*
> *And then you're dead and free from care.*

Now the foolish beetle didn't really feel as sad as you might think if you heard it sing this song. True, the beetle liked to sing the song in a pathetic little voice which quivered and whined as if it was close to death. But the beetle was actually quite content when it was singing. What it liked most was the sound of its own voice, especially when it sounded so pathetic and feeble. From time to time it would stand quite still and stare at its own reflection in a puddle on the forest floor. It would shake its head slowly from side to side. 'Poor me, poor little me,' it would say in its most sympathetic tones. The beetle kept these sweet words of sympathy all for itself, none of the other creatures had heard the beetle address them in this way although many had greater need of kindness and pity.

The bee-eaters sat high in the branches overhead and kept an eye out for the honey bees. These were beautiful birds who lived and worked together for the common good. Every member had a part to play in the survival of the group. Although the bee-eaters were the natural enemies of the bees, they needed the bees as much as the bees needed the flowers. Every creature in the forest understood this and accepted it as a fact of life. There were creatures to be eaten and creatures who ate, there was something for everyone to eat and every creature could find food if it searched hard enough, but each creature knew itself to be another's dinner. It was as simple as that and everyone knew the rules. Everyone except the foolish beetle of course. The bee-eaters spotted the beetle dash out from a hollow log underneath their nest. They could have eaten the beetle but decided not to. It was so full of bitterness it would give them a cramp, one bird said, and the others laughed. They knew all about the foolish beetle and thought it a little sad that there was one beetle which lacked the wisdom and industry typical of its kind.

The mongoose and weasel who also watched the foolish beetle were not so good natured. Both were members of proud, courageous families, they had high standards and they stuck to them. It was all very well to moan about bad luck, the weasel thought, but to do nothing about it was unforgivable. Weasels are nosy and curious creatures and they like to get to the bottom of a problem. The mongoose was a little more reserved and thoughtful, though no less brave. The mongoose sat in his eternal silence* and wondered what had made the beetle so foolish. The mongoose was very old and had lived in the forest for a very long time. It knew that the beetle's troubles were no worse than those of other creatures. The foolish beetle had its enemies like every forest creature, but its food supply was abundant, its home was secure and its future no more uncertain than anyone else's. The mongoose had seen many beetles come and go in the forest and knew that they were hard-working as a rule. He had a very high opinion of beetles in general, admiring their cooperative spirit. He had often watched a tough pair of beetles shift a dung ball much larger than themselves. They would push and pull from both sides until the ball started to move, then they would roll it off to their pit. This was the sort of behaviour

---

* The mongoose is thought to be deaf. No one could explain why, but this seems to be a common belief among farmers and countrypeople in Egypt.

the mongoose admired, not the moans and complaints of the foolish beetle.

The foolish beetle knew all about the impressive stores of its fellow creatures. The other beetles' pits bulged with fine things and they refilled the pits every day so that their supplies never dwindled. The foolish beetle kept well away from the others and felt inadequate. It was not envious or jealous of the other beetles. It was too full of self-pity to have such complicated emotions. The beetle simply considered itself a victim of bad luck, although in fact it was just foolish. But all creatures can use good luck and bad luck as an excuse for not trying to change their ways. This was true of the foolish beetle. It was not born to be foolish, it just became foolish by worrying about too many things.

One evening when the foolish beetle was returning home alone it had a narrow escape. As usual it was very tired after a long day of rushing around and had found almost nothing good to eat. It was sad and worried because the baby beetles were hungry and would be disappointed. But the foolish beetle was more worried about the big tree by the pond. The leaves on the tree were a strange colour and the foolish beetle was sure that they hadn't been that colour a while ago. What was worse was that the leaves were falling off the tree. The beetle was certain that something was terribly wrong and it would get worse of course. It wasn't a good sign, not a good sign at all! The foolish beetle worried about things like this all the time. Hadn't the water been wetter yesterday? Wasn't the grass greener today? Weren't the rushes taller and thinner than usual? Maybe the sun was getting sick, surely it wasn't always as yellow as this?

The foolish beetle was so preoccupied with its worries that it fell into a big hole. There it lay peering up at the trees far above, its legs waving in the air. It was getting dark and soon it would be night, the time of greatest danger for small forest creatures. Now the foolish beetle really had something to worry about. But instead of thinking of a plan or making an effort to escape, the foolish beetle lay there waving its legs and singing its little song. 'Poor me, poor little me! How unfair! Poor little me, all alone and such a victim of fate . . .'

The foolish beetle quite forgot that it was in danger when it was singing and complaining. The beetle closed its eyes and enjoyed the whine and shake in its voice as it echoed down in the deep hole. The foolish beetle was lost in contemplation of its fine singing voice when a sudden noise disturbed these very foolish thoughts. At the top of the hole was an enormous spider.

The spider rubbed its legs together and looked at the beetle with great interest. Here was a fine supper indeed. 'I am very hungry tonight,' the spider announced. The beetle was terrified and becoming aware that this was the worst luck yet. The foolish beetle became still more foolish with fear: 'I'm very hungry too,' it replied in its most polite voice. The spider was quite surprised, not accustomed to having a conversation with its supper, but it found this creature amusing: 'Are you fat and juicy?' it asked. The beetle was taken aback and felt a bit irritated: 'Of course I'm not fat and juicy, just look at me: I'm thin and hungry. Life is hard and unfair, I have terrible bad luck and can't find enough to eat and you ask me if I'm fat!' Well, as you know, it was a very foolish beetle.

The other creatures had noticed the spider creep into the clearing and were hiding and watching from afar. When they realised what had happened they moved closer. The beetle had been in many dangerous situations before, but this was the worst and surely the last.

Once the foolish beetle had fallen into a pond and had floated upside down like an overturned boat until one of the toads had flicked it out to safety. Back on the bank the foolish beetle had not thanked the kind toad. It had not even noticed the group of concerned creatures which had gathered to try to help it. Once the foolish beetle had chased a grub into a hollow log and got stuck inside. Its body was half in and half out, and its back legs were drumming with frustration against the wood. The beetle was still singing its little song when the bee-eaters took pity on it and hopped up and down on the log until they shook the beetle loose.

On many more occasions one creature or another had saved the foolish beetle, and indeed the beetle had come to rely on the intervention of others, not that it ever thanked anyone.

The beetle *was* grateful of course. The foolish are always grateful for any assistance, but they do not see beyond their own bad luck and learn the value of cooperation. A hundred times a day the beetle failed to change its foolish ways. This time, however, the other creatures could not help. The spider was the most deadly enemy of all, what could anyone do? This time the foolish beetle really was alone.

The insects and toads and snakes all watched and waited to see what would happen next. A lizard, familiar with little boys' torture from the world outside, feared that the spider would torment the foolish beetle for entertainment before the kill. The lizard wanted to try to help but the bee-eaters disagreed: 'The spider is hungry and it won't wait long. Don't die a foolish death yourself trying to save the beetle.' The weasel was arguing with one of the more sympathetic toads: 'That foolish beetle would have been dead years ago if we all hadn't helped it at one time or another. This time I say good riddance!' The kind toad shook its head in sorrow and replied: 'No creature should die from foolishness.' 'Nonsense!' retorted the weasel. 'It will die from selfishness, not foolishness.'

A murmur of agreement came from other creatures who had been following the argument. They thought that the most foolish thing about the foolish beetle was that it lived alone and had never learned the value of working together. Unlike the other beetles in the forest, it had never helped anyone or shared a task. One beetle that had joined the crowd of onlookers added: 'That beetle ignored us. It

considered itself to be a superior victim of fate. That's the
real source of its foolishness. It lived alone and will die
alone. The sad thing is that it will die not knowing that
small forest creatures like us are all united in a common
struggle for survival.'

The discussion went on and on while the poor foolish
beetle lay in the deep hole at the spider's mercy. Curiously,
it had stopped singing the pathetic little song. From time
to time it just sighed: 'Poor me, poor little me,' then it
fell silent again. The spider was teasing and mocking the
beetle, saying cruel things like: 'Poor you? You're not poor,
just stupid! Your babies are the poor ones. They'll be
orphans once I eat you. But I'll make a meal of them later,
don't worry that they'll starve to death after you're gone!'
Meanwhile the spider had spun a thick web between two
trees and was binding the beetle with sticky silken ropes in
order to hoist it out of the hole. The beetle, trussed and
unable to move, was jerked out of the hole and seemed to
fly through the air, then it landed right in the middle of the
web. The spider moved quickly and stretched the beetle
out on the web as if it was a rug to be dried in the sun. The
creatures all gasped in horror, then fell silent at a sudden
rustle of leaves. There at the edge of the clearing were the
seven baby beetles.

The creatures were seized with alarm. If the spider
noticed, it would have a ready-made feast prepared with
no effort required. The baby beetles saw their mother in
the web and started to cry. They were very hungry, very
scared and very lonely. The foolish beetle heard their cries
and began to struggle. It had never struggled like this
before, nor had it felt such a sense of urgency or impending
doom. For the first time in its long and foolish life the beetle
was aware that its fate lay in its own hands. The spider
grinned an evil grin, enjoying the sight of another victim
exhausting itself in a useless attempt to escape.

The creatures went on watching. Now they began to
regret the unkind comments they had made about the

foolish beetle. They began to wonder if they might be able to save the foolish beetle or its babies. They began to wish they had not stopped to watch this terrible sight. The foolish beetle still fought against the web and started to roar with fury and fear. What a sound it made! It was a mighty roar full of anguish and determination and love of life. The roar had a tone quite different from the pathetic little song. The beetle called out to the babies below: 'My poor children! Flee! Save yourselves and don't despair!' It caught sight of the spider moving closer, grinning a still more evil grin. The end was near.

Afterwards no one was sure of the exact sequence of events, but something like this happened. There had been a final roar from the beetle, then a thunderous sound from high above in the roof of the forest. Out of nowhere came a huge white bird. The bird hovered high above them, beating its enormous wings, then it swooped towards the forest floor. It fell like a stone. The trees shook and there was a great wind which blew up like a sudden storm.

The terrified creatures watched in amazement. The great white bird soared again, then it dived between the two trees, smashing the spider's web. The cruel strands of silk which had imprisoned the beetle were scattered. As the broken strands of the web sailed to the forest floor, the foolish beetle clung to one and landed with a clumsy bump on top of a big pile of dung. The spider was nowhere to be seen. It seemed that the great bird had scooped it up in its beak and swallowed it whole. All the creatures cheered as the beetle was reunited with its family. The babies jumped up and down, crowding around their mother as they comforted each other.

Everyone looked up to the tree tops at the sound of flapping wings as the huge white bird came down to land on a high branch. It began to speak in a big booming voice: 'Forest creatures, you have seen a thing which will not be seen again, so remember it and learn from it.'

All the creatures huddled together, both excited and

fearful at the sight of this mighty bird. No one spoke, even the babblers* didn't dare to chatter but sat in silence looking like serious if untidy hermits.

However, the foolish beetle had no such reservations. The beetle looked straight up at the great bird and said: 'Great white bird, you have saved my life and permitted me to return to my children. I cannot find the words to thank you! I do not know how to thank you! Thank you! Thank you! I do not know how to thank you! I am overcome with gratitude!' The beetle had been about to continue but the bird interrupted: 'Listen and remember what I have said,' it boomed. 'This day you have all been a witness to a lesson about life. See that you learn from it.' With those words the bird spread its vast wings and soared far above the trees out of sight.

The forest creatures scanned the sky but the great bird was gone. No doubt it would never be seen again. It was not a bird of the forest or a bird of the ocean, they all knew that it was a creature from the kingdom of magic. Now it was almost dark. The night in the forest is a dangerous time and everyone began to leave the clearing for the safety of their homes. They took their leave of the beetle and wished it a safe and peaceful night. Each creature departed in deep thought, searching for a personal lesson it might learn from the event as the great bird had ordered.

Alone with its babies in the clearing, the foolish beetle noticed the dung heap where it had landed with such a bump. It worked on a loose lump and began rolling it along, calling for the babies to follow. The little band made their way home, picking up scraps of food here and there as if it had been raining good things to eat. The foolish beetle had never had such luck with foraging for food. But

---

* Babblers are a common species of bird in Southern Egypt. They live up to their name, usually being found in roving bands chattering incessantly. This, together with their long tails and rather scraggy plumage, gives them an amusing rakish air. Babblers often have a comic role in tales or are portrayed as daft gossips who misunderstand events and bring about a comedy of errors.

late that night, when the baby beetles were fast asleep and the forest was still, a quiet voice broke the silence. It was a pathetic little voice which quivered and whined: 'Ah poor me, poor little me. So alone and such a victim of fate.'

Oum Ali sighed and gasped her way through the tale as usual. She gave no indication that it was received in a different spirit from any other tale. This was not lost on the rest of the company. Few of us could resist frequent glances at Oum Ali whenever the Foolish Beetle's little refrain was chanted. Everyone found the tale very funny, until the final twist when it seemed that the beetle had lost the chance to reform. Oum Ali was the first to tut with exasperation at this point. She had much to say in praise of the tale and was keen to fill any gap in the general chat with more news of Ali's ill health before she left. Amira and I overheard the following whispered exchange between Oum Idris and Oum Karim as we walked home behind them:

Oum Idris: 'It's funny how people can listen but don't hear anything.'
Oum Karim: 'I think it's very sad, I felt sorry for that poor creature.'
Oum Idris: 'Nonsense! I'm more sorry for her poor children!'

Amira and I shared the guilty look of unwilling eavesdroppers. We had nothing to say. There was no way of telling if they were discussing the Foolish Beetle or Oum Ali.

OUM KARIM: A HOPEFUL WOMAN

Oum Karim sits in a corner of the room, leaning against the wall. During the evening two of her children tuck themselves under an arm on each side of her cushion and her baby is passed from one lap to another. From time to time it seems as if Oum Karim has fallen asleep. She has her eyes closed and her breathing becomes slow and regular, especially when a tale is long and complex. But she can be as alert as everyone else if the suspense mounts or the tale reaches an exciting conclusion. Sometimes one of her perceptive remarks about a tale firmly contradicts this general inattentive appearance. Oum Karim always looks frail and ill. She is a clever and observant young woman, but by the end of most evenings she has sunk into an exhausted stupor. The reasons for this are clear from the story of her life.

Although I am married and with four young children I have a job at home to earn money. People may say that this is wrong or shameful but it's a fact of my life. Sometimes people don't like to see how many women like me there are. Perhaps we're so ashamed and afraid about what people say that we try to keep our work out of sight. I just wish that I didn't feel so tired and worn out. I'm just twenty-four but I feel like an old woman at times. But I've never expected life to be easy and I don't like to complain.

I'm hopeful that my children will have a better life, although I'm not sure if I will live to see it. I'm not surprised by the number of problems which occur in the city, poor people are always at the bottom of the heap and so they have most problems. But I grew up knowing all about this. My mother was unhappy and hated the city because she had expected everything to be different, so as a child I learned not to expect too much. I suppose I'm lucky because I didn't have to learn the hard way like my mother.

I was born in this neighbourhood the year after my

parents left their small village near Qena.* My father had
to give up his land after he lost a dispute with a big lan-
downer about water rights. I don't think he was a wealthy
farmer but he made a decent living, at least he did his best
until he had to move because there was no water. I know
about this as if I'd been there myself because my mother
talked about it all the time. She said the move to the city
was a tragedy, a move of desperation, that's how she
always described it.

My parents came here because my father had a second
cousin who had migrated some years earlier. I can't
remember him very clearly, although we lived with his
family until my youngest sister was born. I think that
arrangement lasted for about five years. I was the first child
born in the city, then there was a baby who died at birth,
then my sister Laila. My father's relatives helped him to
find work and he had several jobs. He worked very long
hours and was very tired when he came home. None of the
jobs paid well and he could only get casual work, so he used
to come home with a new job every few weeks.

My mother was really upset and frightened by the
insecurity of his employment. She had to take a job to boost
my father's income and that changed her life and her
outlook on life completely. My mother had never liked the
city and was very homesick because she missed her family.
She felt that having to take a job was the final blow. It
destroyed her spirit completely and I don't think I ever saw
her smile or laugh again. She knew that they'd never be
wealthy enough to get back to the village, I think that had
been her secret dream in the early days here.

I was about five or six when I first realised that we were
poor. I remember asking my mother for something to eat

---

* Oum Karim's parents came from a village in the Eastern Desert territory
which stretches from the Nile to the Red Sea. Qena, the nearest big town, lies
along the east bank of the Nile about sixty miles north of Luxor.

because I was hungry and she slapped me. I was so surprised that I didn't even cry, but when I went to look in the cupboard later it was empty. This memory has stayed with me since then and I don't care if I half-starve myself, but I'll never refuse my own children food or let them find an empty cupboard. You see, my mother hated having to work so much that it changed her completely. She used to say that my father had caused all her problems by leaving the village, and that they had lost everything and gained nothing. That was unfair because what choice did they have? It wasn't as if my father invented poverty, every city has its poor people! One of my mother's favourite sayings was: life in the city promises you riches, but we've got only rags. All these years later I can still hear her voice when I think of my childhood.

I had four more sisters and brothers when I was still a young girl and I remember playing with them and having fun like children everywhere. It wasn't at all sad and it didn't seem like a life of hardship to us, because we were children. I had just started to cover my hair when things began to look up for our family.*

Relatives of my father had made some money and they invested it in a vegetable stall. My father started to run this stall and was quite successful. The big problem was that my mother had to work with him. Until then mother had worked from home, and although she'd hated this, she hated outside work even more. After she had to work in the streets she took it as a sign that they'd gone down in the world. My father insisted that it was just a temporary thing, and after a while she wouldn't have to work at all,

---

* Girls usually begin to cover their hair with a scarf or veil at puberty. At this time there are also restrictions imposed on a girl's movements outside the house without a guardian or chaperone. Oum Karim recalled that she was about eleven when her mother told her that she was 'no longer a child' and had to start 'behaving like a woman'. In Oum Karim's particular case she remembers being to told to cover her hair, to avoid meeting and talking to all unrelated men and to stop playing outside.

but of course this never happened. I think that my mother considered a female vegetable seller to be little better than a prostitute.

My mother never forgave my father for taking her away from the village as long as she lived. I remember that she always dressed in black as if someone had died. When I was little I once asked her about her clothes and she told me that she was in mourning for her own village kin, they were dead as far as she was concerned because she would never see them again. That gives you some idea of what my mother was like. She didn't believe that you should keep your feelings to yourself. My father suffered most, I suppose, because she never let him forget that he had brought her to the city but failed to take proper care of her.

It's difficult for me to understand why a country upbringing affects people so deeply. I know my parents both yearned to return, but they couldn't afford the trip and they had no land to go back to anyway. I think it was the dream of returning which was most important to them both. I was about thirteen when my mother died and I overheard her last words to my father. She said something like: 'You had all those plans and dreams over the years but I had just one, to get back home.'

My father was heartbroken when she died and I think he blamed himself for her death. He gathered all the children around him before the funeral and asked us if we wanted to live in a village. What an impossible question. Of course we didn't know, we'd never even seen a village and so we didn't know what to say. But I think that my father wasn't really speaking to us, he was just saying this out of loyalty to mother, as if he could please mother's ghost more easily than he'd pleased her when she was alive. Naturally we didn't move back to the village, we couldn't have moved anywhere because there was no money.

In any case I suspect that my father didn't want to leave the city, because it would have been like an admission of failure. He was ashamed that his move to the city had not brought him riches. I remember that he always became anxious when someone from his village or home region arrived in the neighbourhood in case they would say that he hadn't done very well for himself. He was afraid that news would get back to his village and old friends would know that he was worse off after his move to the city.

But my father tried hard to take care of us as long as he lived, and I know that things could have been much worse. He managed to build more permanent rooms for us and pay off his loan before he died. Both of these things were major achievements and they were his greatest ambitions in life. He died two years after mother and then my oldest brother became head of the family. Things were pretty hard then for all of us.

My brothers continued to sell vegetables and my sisters and I started to take in sewing work at home. We struggled on like this for about two years and each one of us did our bit for the family. My baby brother even ran errands for the tailor and was very proud of the penny or two he was able to contribute. It wasn't such a terrible time as you might imagine, in fact I remember it as one of the happiest times of my life. We were all young and full of hope. We had the kind of closeness that grows out of common hardship, and that makes up for a lot. My brothers' main worry was about my marriage. I had to have a husband but there wasn't much money available to spend on a wedding.

The relative who helped my father when he came to the city introduced my brother to the man I was to marry and they made an agreement which didn't involve much cash. At that time I took a job in a workshop because I could earn a lot more there. I saved to buy household things and made a contribution to the cost of my wedding. Ahmed, the man I married, had family ties in my parents' home village and this made the marriage arrangements easier because there is mutual trust between people from the same area. My brothers and my husband's family made a trading agreement which cemented the marriage arrangements. Ahmed's father was a fruit and vegetable seller, and my brothers agreed to pool supplies and resources with Ahmed's family in the future. That sorted out the economic side of things and the wedding feast took place just after my seventeenth birthday.

I knew Ahmed a little before the wedding, we had met a few times when his mother invited me to their home. He seemed very nice, at least that was the impression of an innocent girl of seventeen. How can you really know a man you've just met, you have to become his wife before you understand him.

We began married life together in two small rooms which belonged to his family. They weren't far from my former home and so it didn't seem that much had changed. Ahmed continued to work on the stall and took other part-time jobs to earn a bit more money. I gave up my job at the workshop when we got married and looked after the house. I had two sons in a little over two years and these were the happiest years of my marriage. We always had a bit of a struggle with money, but I didn't have to take a job. It was wonderful to be able to keep house and look after the babies without having to work at the same time. But before my second son was a year old things got so bad that I had to find some way of earning money again.

This is the thing that finally made me understand my mother's despair and anger. I'm stuck in this position I hate and I know that it isn't likely to change. The saddest thing is that I'm missing so much of my children's early years and I can't take time to play with them as much as I'd like to because of my job. It really breaks my heart to have to send the children outside when I'd much rather spend time with them than work for the dressmaker.

The dressmaker pays me for cutting out patterns and tacking the garments together. She doesn't have the time to do this herself and she finds it a bother because she gets bad pains in her hands. It's not difficult work and I can cut out a dress when the children are sleeping or playing outside. The money helps with the cost of keeping house and I try to save a little for the boys' education and for medicine in case they fall ill. But it's not easy and my savings don't amount to much because I've rarely more than a penny or two left over each week.

The dressmaker expects me to have an order finished in a day. She sends the fabric and instructions over to the house and if it's something simple then there's no problem. But if she needs the work done quickly, or if the pattern is quite complicated, I find it really difficult to get the job done in time. Then I worry that she'll be angry, or won't pay me on time or even send the work to somebody else. As I said, the worst problem is finding the time to work and not neglecting all the other things I have to do.

Caring for the children takes so much time because there are always things they want me to do. They need me to fix their toys or tell stories or play games, and of course it takes a lot of time to do the cooking and washing properly. I sometimes wish I could split myself into pieces in order to get everything done. But we need the money I earn, so it's a matter of making time for everything. Still, I would never let my work interfere with caring for the children. That would be a crime against my husband and the little ones, as well as a dishonour on my father's house and myself. But I live in hope that I'll get better at my work and be able to finish each task faster, that way I'll have more time to devote to the children.

The amount I earn depends on the type of garment I have to cut out. A simple dress with a straight skirt and sleeves earns less than a more complicated one with pleats and gathers. It's a bit difficult to explain because it also depends on the type of fabric. But it's a fair system of payment because you earn what you deserve according to the time spent on the job. I mean, a heavy expensive fabric takes ages to cut out, especially when you think how much it's worth and you're afraid of ruining it! One thing that's difficult with this type of work is not knowing exactly how much you'll earn. It all depends on the number of orders the dressmaker has, so my wages aren't reliable or secure. But I can't complain since the work suits me. A job with regular wages involves working set hours away from home and that's just not possible.

If I couldn't work from home I wouldn't be able to earn money at all. I even prefer to work on the cotton garments which pay the least, as long as I have enough of them to earn a reasonable sum. They don't take too long to finish, and they don't get in the way of housework or looking after the children. I also worry a lot less about cotton than expensive fabric. If I have metres of expensive stuff around the house I feel sick with panic in case the children soil it or I make a mistake when I'm cutting it out. How could I replace it? The price of a length of velvet would feed us for weeks!

Ahmed is a good husband but he's never been able to make enough money to provide for all our needs. His wages don't cover food costs let alone the usual things that young children need, like shoes and clothes. When I gave up work just after we married I was foolish enough to think that I wouldn't have to find another job. Of course I was ignorant about a lot of things in those days, especially the fact that life gets harder as you grow up. We were often hungry when the babies were young and so I gradually realised that I would have to earn money to help my husband out. It's not that I was greedy for money like some people are, we just needed money for basic things, it was money to live! That was when I asked the dressmaker if she had any tasks I could do, that was the start of my new working life.

This work of mine is the thing that has caused the greatest problems in my marriage. It would be better if Ahmed didn't know that I worked because then he wouldn't feel so bad about it. At first I tried to keep my job secret because I knew how angry he would be. There were a lot of harsh words when he found out about it. I'd been working for some months when he noticed some sewing I'd forgotten to put away and asked me what it was. I was stupid enough to tell him, but after that first fight he never mentioned it again and that was almost three years ago.

I try to keep whatever I'm working on hidden in a special basket so that he won't see it and feel embarrassed or angry. The sad thing is that he's more angry with himself than he is with me. This is because he can't provide for his family and so he feels like a bad father and husband. It's strange that a man who is angry with himself always takes it out on his wife. As I said, it's vital to keep all signs of my work hidden from Ahmed. It's better like this and perhaps in time he can come to believe that everything is fine and as it should be.

When I get my money from the dressmaker the first thing I do is to spend a few hours at the market buying food. I'm extra careful about what I buy and always get exactly the same things as Ahmed buys. If he brings home a particular brand of rice and macaroni, I buy an extra supply of the same type of rice and macaroni. That way it looks like he buys all the food in our cupboard, although in truth the groceries he buys last less than a week. After my wages have boosted our food store we've enough food to last until his next pay packet, and Ahmed can think that he provides all our meals himself. Ahmed probably suspects that I buy food in secret but he'd never mention it.

It's better to ignore difficult things like this, and I think we can cope with this situation as long as Ahmed can pretend that everything is as it should be. It would be too hurtful and complicated to reprimand me for this trick. I only deceive Ahmed because I think it's for the best, it would be too unkind to make a show of the fact that he fails in his duty to look after the family's needs. This way he can pretend that he is a real man and a proper father and husband. There are few men in this area who don't live with the same kind of pretence. You see, if a man can't provide for his own family, then somehow he's less than a proper man. It's considered a deeply shameful thing between a husband and wife, especially the wife who has to help make money. It doesn't seem to make much sense when you try to explain it, but that's just how things are.

Of course it's wrong to deceive your husband, but what else can a wife do? It's like one wrong thing leads to another. I don't think it's right that a wife and mother should work, and I don't think it's right to trick your husband, but these two things are linked together. I often criticise myself and feel ashamed because there's so much deceit in my life, but I still hope that things will get better. I can't help thinking that as long as I fulfil my duty as Ahmed's wife and the mother of his children, then he should be content. But he seems to feel so inadequate because he can't earn enough to look after us. That makes him cross all the time, and it's rare for anything to please him.

People here don't have easy lives and I think women have the worst problems to cope with. But what mother could watch her children starve? Of course it would be perfect if I could devote all my time to my children. If I didn't have to work I'd throw away the patterns and scissors and spend all day playing with the children and cooking and cleaning. Although it seems that I hate my job, I'm not really complaining about it. My job isn't the worst problem, but it's the time that it takes which causes the problems. All that sewing leaves me with little time for the things I'd really love to be doing. I often feel like crying when the little ones are begging me to tell another story but I can't spare the time because the dressmaker is expecting me to have an order ready by the following morning. I hate feeling tired all the time as well. I suppose it's unavoidable, because I have to work through the night to finish off garments, although I shouldn't moan about it. One good thing is that I can keep scraps of fabric and I make toys and puppets from these left-over odds and ends. If I sew until dawn I can have a surprise waiting for the children when they wake up.

I try not to feel torn apart by guilt and fear that I might be neglecting my children, but of course it's a problem. My only excuse is that I have to work, otherwise we'd go hungry. This way of life is often criticised by more fortunate women, but what else would they do in my situation? I would do anything in the world for my children, whatever the risk or disgrace. My hope in the future keeps me going and it gets me through the days when I really hate my working life. My greatest hope of all is that my daughters won't have to live like this. I'll work until I drop if it means that my daughters won't have to choose between their work and their children. If I can find them good husbands with good prospects, then I'll die happy. I expect that my own mother hoped that things would be better for me, but maybe she didn't have a strong enough hope for the future.

Oum Karim was quiet and subdued on the evening when the following tale was told. She appeared to be less willing than usual to take part in any conversation and ate very little, although Amira and Oum Mohmmed made a great effort to ply her with food. I knew that Oum Karim had had a serious argument with her husband earlier that day, because I had been visiting them. But such rows were not uncommon and it seemed an insufficient reason to explain her very low spirits. The other women were aware of this and tried to cheer her up. Whatever the cause of Oum Karim's depression and despite our concern for her, no one expected the following tale or anticipated its impact.

THE HIDDEN TREASURE

This is a tale of a secret which was not a secret at all.

Once there was a little girl who lived in a poor home with her poor family. They had barely enough to eat and her clothes were always in rags. Her mother was a good woman but beaten down by the struggle against hardship.

She had become obsessed with finding enough food for her children and with her own problems. She forgot that little girls need some happiness and fun when they are young. The child was serious and lived in a make-believe world of huge magical animals who followed her through the streets as she went about her chores, gazing at her with big friendly eyes. Although she was a solitary child, she never felt alone, and when she was sad her imaginary friends would cheer her up.

One day the little girl was sent to the pump to fetch the buckets of water her mother needed. It was still early and the sun was not yet high. The little girl took the Big One with her, the huge bear-like beast which was a frequent companion. He waddled at her heels making little snorting and grunting noises, surprising sounds for such an enormous creature. This was the time of day when the little girl was most happy. There were few arguments and angry words at home at this time of the morning. Her mother started each day in a spirit of quiet resignation, and rarely succumbed to utter despair and furious self-pity before midday.

The little girl and her invisible friend took the long route to the pump, heedless of time and domestic concerns. They passed the baker's home and the neat shop front of the dressmaker, and then they turned the final corner and crossed the square. At this early hour the square was already crammed with the stalls of vendors who sold hot snacks, nuts, sewing kits, fruit and sweets, plastic sandals, matches and a hundred and one other things besides. The little girl loved the square when it was ringing with vendors' cries on days like this. She would peep shyly at each stall and feast her eyes on the wonderful array of goods for sale. But the little girl did not desire the wonderful things she saw. She had no wish to possess anything in particular, not even a small item from the toy seller's gaudy stall, like one of the unusual mechanical dogs which barked and bounced when you wound them up. A quick peep was enough for this little girl, although she had no toys of her own because her mother could not afford them. She was immune from the greed which often afflicts the poorest of people. She was content with her make-believe world and the familiar company of her greatest friend, the Big One.

Remembering the other chores that awaited her, the little girl quickly filled her buckets at the pump and hurried back in the direction of her home. The streets were filling up now as people hurried to work, or to the market, or to the square itself to wash clothes and fill buckets. The little girl was glad that she had been there before the others, that way she would not have to stop and engage in polite conversation about difficult family affairs.

The Big One ambled along at her side, pointing out things of interest and grunting in his curious muffled voice in response to her questions. He was a wise beast and the little girl liked to confide in him and ask him about things which worried or puzzled her. 'Why are some people poor and others rich?' was a question she often asked. The Big One always chuckled before he answered and he never gave the same explanation twice. One day he would say: 'Because God wants the poor people to show the rich the error of their ways.' Another time he would explain: 'We live in a strange world and must accept what fate offers us.' Yet another answer was: 'Because the poor have more gifts than the rich, but they must learn to recognise that.'

This time the Big One gave the following response and asked the little girl: 'What is rich and what is poor? Can't poor people be rich and rich people poor?' Although the Big One often said mysterious things and spoke in riddles, the little girl thought that this was the most curious thing her friend had ever said. She turned his questions around in her head and tried to work out what to say. After a minute she replied: 'That's easy, poor people can be rich if they find a fortune or buried treasure, or discover a secret hoard of gold and jewels, and of course rich people can lose their money or it can be stolen or . . .' The little girl was

pleased with this clever response and she smiled at the Big
One, happy that she had found an answer to his riddle. She
was surprised when the creature grinned at her. He shook
his great shaggy head: 'Only a clever girl can say such
stupid things,' he teased.

They had stopped under a thin tree at the edge of the
rubbish dump. The smell of rotting food and waste was
overpowering as the day grew hotter. Hundreds of busy
flies hovered and settled on the choicest scraps in search of
a tasty meal. The Big One pointed to a fat fly. 'Look at
him,' he said. 'Now is he a rich fly or is he a poor one?' The
little girl giggled at the thought of a rich fly family. They
would wear fancy clothes and eat off linen-covered tables.
Their children would have mechanical toys like wind-up
dogs which barked and bounced. The magical creature
could read her thoughts and he smiled too. The Big One
began strolling around the dump and the little girl followed
him. Now and then he bent over and poked about in the
piles of rubbish.

The little girl watched in fascination as she caught sight
of the treasure the Big One was revealing to her. It must
have have been buried in the rubbish. There were clumps
of rubies and emeralds, caches of gold and silver trinkets
and bundles of banknotes. The Big One uncovered each
thing for just a second, then pushed it deep into the pile
again. The rubies and trinkets and banknotes disappeared
from view, hidden underneath rotten cabbage leaves and
orange peel.

At last the Big One straightened his enormous back and
stood up slowly. He lifted a stick which lay against the tree
and handed it to the little girl. She took it and looked at
him curiously, unsure what he wanted her to do with the
stick. The Big One gave her a solemn bow, followed by a
quick wink: 'You try now,' he said, pointing to the rubbish
dump with a grand gesture. The little girl was enjoying this
game and she returned the courtly bow. 'All these riches
shall be thine!' boomed the Big One in his funniest voice.

The little girl copied the movements the beast had made
as she circled the mound of rubbish and poked at it with
the stick. It was a good game. She speared a mouldy sweet
potato which had gone soft in the middle and offered it to
the Big One: 'A fine, fresh mango, my Lord, straight from
far-off shores!' she proclaimed. With a wave of his paw the
Big One transformed the potato, and its rough purplish
skin really did become smooth and greeny-gold like a ripe
mango. The little girl stuck the mango back in the rubbish
heap and it turned into a rotten potato again.

The little girl continued to play and poke around in the
piles of rubbish. This time she turned over some charred
paper and there, underneath, was a silver necklace set with
sapphires. She was stunned by the beauty of this thing.
She had never dreamed that such an exquisite object could
exist, even the jewels uncovered by the Big One had not
been so splendid. The Big One gave a growl of anticipation:
'Would the fine young lady take this necklace as a token
of her worth?' he asked. The little girl jumped as if startled
by the suddenness of the question. She gave him a swift,
curious look with the eyes of a much older, wiser individual. Finally she shook her head mischievously, becoming
a simple little girl again. 'Alas my Lord,' she began, 'I must
not accept this token; while it is most beauteous, it is not
properly mine and I am not worthy of it.' The little girl
turned back to the dump and continued to churn up the
rubbish with her stick. She uncovered another stack of
burned paper and the necklace disappeared from view.
The beast bowed to her again in the grand style he had
assumed, then in his more usual manner he grinned and
ruffled her hair in affectionate approval.

The little girl was in a new section of the dump. A book
was lying on the surface and she reached for it, careful not
to lose her balance and fall into the stinking mess. It was
a very tatty old book, its cover was stained and many of
the pages had been torn out. The little girl couldn't read,
so she had no idea what the book was about. She couldn't

imagine where it had come from because hardly anybody in this neighbourhood had books. The few families who did took extra-special care of such rare items and they would never throw one away. Still, it was an interesting thing so she put down the stick and took the book over to the Big One. She sat down beside him in the shade of the tree and they examined it together. Although there were few printed pages which remained intact, the little girl looked at each one with interest. But at the very back of the book she discovered a lovely picture, about the size of a post-card, which someone had glued to the inside cover. .

It was a colourful picture and the little girl loved it. She stared at it, considering every figure in detail and investigating every corner of the scene. There was a ship about to set sail in a busy harbour. It was a fine cloudless day, the sky was a brilliant blue which matched the sea, and the bright sun made the ocean shimmer. There were hundreds of people crowding together on the quayside, perhaps waiting to board the ship, perhaps seeing friends off on an important voyage, perhaps simply there for the fun and excitement of such an occasion. Passengers were standing on a high deck, far above the crowd. The little girl was especially interested in them. There was a woman surrounded by small children right at the front of the deck and they were waving to the people below. One girl who stood next to her mother had a red scarf which was fluttering in the breeze. Everyone looked very happy.

It was a lovely picture indeed and the little girl wanted to discuss it with the Big One. She carefully peeled the picture off the cover of the book and tucked it into the deep pocket of her dress. Then she took the old book to the rubbish pile and threw it far into the centre of the dump site. She stood watching the book fly through the air and land with a bump which disturbed a swarm of busy flies. A harsh slap from behind interrupted the little girl's thoughts and she felt her cheek stinging and grow hot and pink. There was her mother in a terrible temper, shaking her fists. The Big One had disappeared, no doubt hiding in case he might somehow provoke the girl's mother to greater anger. The little girl looked down in shame and fear. She had lost all track of time inside her secret world.

She was useless and lazy and worthless! She was disobedient and stupid! She had forgotten about the buckets of water and preferred to play on the rubbish heap like an animal! Oh, and she was selfish too! She didn't know the extent of her mother's troubles, she never thought of the struggle her mother had to keep greedy mouths full! She was ungrateful! She didn't deserve any kindness, she was bad news, a waste of space! The sooner she got married and went off the better, though who would marry such a lazy, thoughtless, good-for-nothing girl.

The little girl listened to the flood of wrath which flew from her mother's lips, each exclamation finishing with another slap. She did not flinch, but stood there waiting for it to end as she always did. Finally, her mother grew quite exhausted from her outburst, turned on the spot and marched towards the house. The little girl, her face glowing from embarrassment and the slaps, lifted the heavy buckets and followed as quickly as she could.

Late that same night she lay curled up on her bed roll. Her sisters were fast asleep beside her and there was utter silence in the room except for the regular breathing of the other children. Her mother had not spoken to her since the outburst that morning, and had not given her a plate at dinner time. The little girl said nothing, and her brothers and sisters didn't ask why she was going hungry, each one secretly pleased that there was a little more food to help fill their own empty stomachs. In any case, when the woman of the house was in a temper no one dared to question her. The punishments she imposed were absolute and accepted in silence.

The sad child thought about the Big One as she lay awake that night. She hoped that he was not angry with her too. She was afraid that he would agree with her

mother that she was lazy and worthless and refuse to see
her again. She reached into her pocket and took out the
picture. She had been too scared to look at it earlier in case
her mother would spy it and and destroy it. Her mother
hated anything that could be associated with dirt, having
spent her whole life fighting a losing battle against it.

The picture looked just as lovely in the moonlight which
shone into the tiny room, but a little more mysterious. The
ocean which stretched far into the distance seemed to be
moving. The little girl thought that she could see the sails
of the ship fluttering. The happy family on the top deck
were looking out of the picture at her and the smiling
daughter flapped her red scarf in a friendly wave. The little
girl fell asleep with the picture tucked safely under her
pillow and dreamed of future happiness.

Now the little girl is grown up and has a family of her
own. What future happiness did she find? She did not
escape to a lovely world of blue skies, riches and freedom
from toil of course.

The storyteller paused for just a moment, waiting for the women
to settle down so she could be heard over our collective groans.
All emotions were running high as the tale had unfolded. Everyone had been enchanted, amused, then saddened in quick succes-
sion. Most of the women had been moved to tears, even the
cynical Oum Idris had wiped her eyes from time to time. Oum
Karim had been leaning against the wall in her usual position
with her eyes closed, but I sensed she was uneasy. Although
she appeared relaxed she was breathing very quickly. An occa-
sional, involuntary jerk betrayed the fact of her growing distress. A spontaneous ripple of sighs rose in the tiny room and
did not fade away as the storyteller continued to describe the
heroine's struggle.

No, of course the woman did not escape to a world of riches
and freedom from toil. People rarely do except in fairy
tales, and this is no fairy tale.

This woman has children of her own and she is the best

mother in the world. She loves them and cares for them
with all her heart and strength. She finds it a joy to amuse
her little ones and she thrills them with stories about fantastic creatures who befriend sad lonely children and show
them magical things.

The man of the house is well cared for and this good
woman takes satisfaction in trying to make him comfortable. Life is not easy for this husband and wife, but the
woman is resourceful and clever and puts her best efforts
into every task whether it is pleasant or not. She tries to
make the family home as happy a place as possible and is
sure to bury anything that might cause offence. There is
no evidence of anger or discontent in her home. But this
is not the only thing she is keen to keep hidden . . .

The tale was interrupted by a piercing cry from Oum Karim
which sounded like 'It's not true!', then she ran out of the room
sobbing. It was clear from everyone's faces that this was a terrible unprecedented incident. The storyteller, pale and tearful,
was shaking her head in apparent despair; we all were. Oum
Mohammed and Amira immediately went after Oum Karim.
We could hear murmuring voices as they tried to comfort her
behind the curtain.

After a few minutes Oum Karim came back on her escorts'
arms. Our stunned silence in the dark room during her absence
had made it seem much longer. Amira sat next to her and Oum
Karim's children filled both their laps. Oum Karim had her face
buried in the little boys' hair. She apologised for interrupting
the tale without looking up and said that she felt better. Oum
Mohammed produced more refreshments and we emptied
another huge pot of tea and plate of cakes before the atmosphere
began to lighten. The storyteller offered to start another tale, a
short jolly one she said, but we wanted to hear the first one out.
Oum Karim joined our wary requests to finish the tale of the
Hidden Treasure.

So what is this thing which the good woman keeps hidden?
The woman has a secret source of happiness tucked away.
She keeps an old postcard in the bottom of her sewing box.

It is a rather faded picture, a bit creased and curled at the corners, but still a lovely picture. When she is sad, which is quite often, although she tries not to be, she takes out this old treasure and gazes at the scene. She is no longer a little girl with the simple concerns and fears of childhood, but a good mother in a difficult world.

The woman closes her eyes and recreates the picture in her mind. There on the deck of the splendid ship she sees herself laughing and waving. Beside her, the happy children hang over the rails, shaking their scarfs and hankies to the crowd below. Before them is the excitement of a journey to a far-off land where there is no hunger and sadness.

In the past she had struggled and suffered in the hope of future happiness, but now at last she can rest. The woman echoes her children's excited cries because everything has turned out as she planned. She has been dreaming of this journey for a very long time.

It had been a very strange evening of unexpected actions and emotional upset. Oum Karim looked up for the first time and gave a shaky but sincere smile. It did not seem to be directed to anyone in particular, more a general signal that she had recovered her characteristic composure. This was a good time to leave and nobody seemed interested in lingering last-minute gossip. Amira walked home with Oum Karim and I helped wash Oum Mohammed's best dishes and made polite conversation until Amira returned. We called to see Oum Karim just before midnight. She was busy sewing while the children and her husband slept, but insisted on making us tea. We drank quickly, relieved that she seemed more cheerful and not wanting to disturb her work further. As we left the house Amira reminded me of the last line of the tale: 'She has been dreaming for a very long time.' It was a barely audible whisper but we all heard it and Oum Karim responded with what looked like a nod of agreement.

The following evening when there was a call for a tale, the storyteller was less than eager to respond. An unusual silence descended on the company of women as we remembered how

upset Oum Karim had been after last night's tale. Perhaps she
would say something to break the atmosphere of collective discomfort? The storyteller looked to Oum Karim for some hint of
consent to another tale. Oum Karim nodded, then placed her
hand on her youngest son's head. 'Tell the story of the young
sultan's quest,' she said, 'it's young Ahmed's favourite.' Oum
Mohammed was fond of this story too; she smiled and began to
tell the popular folk tale.

THE YOUNG SULTAN'S QUEST

Once there was a great and good sultan. He had cellars
filled with gold and precious jewels, his kitchens were
crammed full of good things to eat, he lived with his beautiful wife in an enormous palace with elaborate gardens
and he had seven beautiful daughters. His life was complete except for one thing. The sultan's problem was that
he had no sons. This sad fact hung over his life like a storm
cloud and he wanted a son more than anything else in the
world. The sultan was a wise man and he believed that you
have to give in order to receive, so he gave hundreds of gold
pieces to the needy and built a great mosque to the glory
of God with a minaret of silver and turquoise. After this,
the sultan's beautiful wife gave birth to a son and the
palace resounded with cheers and thanksgiving for many
weeks.

The little boy, called Ahmad, was surrounded by so
many adoring people that he grew up spoiled and rather
unpleasant. His father, mother, seven sisters and all the
courtiers granted his every wish, so the older he grew
the nastier he became. By the age of sixteen Ahmad was a
very handsome, but troublesome and selfish, young man.
Another problem was that he had no idea of thrift or careful spending. After the old sultan died, the young prince
began to spend money as if the palace coffers were bottomless. The extravagant young man bought great horses,
enough to seat an army. The amount of fabric used in all
the rich new robes he ordered would have clothed half

the men in the kingdom. He bought racing camels and diamonds as big as eggs. But he soon tired of all these things and forgot about them, leaving the horses and camels in the charge of careless servants and losing his cloaks and jewels in odds corners of the palace.

In a short time the vast fortune built up during the late sultan's long and worthy life was halved. The young sultan's mother begged him to use his wealth with caution and to understand the value of money, but he ignored her. His sisters pleaded with him to provide some money for their dowries, but he ignored them as well. Ahmad was so in love with himself that he heard nothing and understood less. He did only what he liked and refused any pursuit that did not bring immediate pleasure. His wealth bought him fun and entertainment, but he lived in blissful ignorance of his own bad behaviour and the needs of others. Before long the courtiers and overseers became disenchanted with Ahmad and were openly critical of the young man they had once spoiled so thoughlessly. He ignored the advice of the wisest courtiers and left the management of the palace and lands in the hands of the most foolish, obsequeious viziers. Secretly the sultana despaired of finding him a wife, such was the dark side of his youthful nature.

One night after a gluttonous feast Ahmad had a curious dream. He saw a shimmering angel at the foot of his bed and the angel's expression made him nervous. The angel addressed him in a golden voice and its message made his heart grow cold: 'All good things must come to an end. Even a bottomless well runs dry. No pleasure is so great that it does not die.' Ahmed did not understand these wise words or connect them with his own faults, but he could not overlook the note of warning in the angel's voice. He sat up in bed and spoke to the angel in a commanding tone: 'What do you want? Don't talk in riddles, speak clearly!' But Ahmad was frightened and the force of his imperious words was diminished because his voice shook. He even added 'please'. Then the angel repeated its warning and

said: 'All good things must come to an end. Now listen!
You must go to the great city of Damascus in the northern
lands. There you will find an old sage called Ramadan. He
will send you off on a quest for your heart's desire.' Ahmad
was intrigued and forgot his fright. 'What is my heart's
desire?' he asked eagerly. The angel shook its head as if
thinking a secret thought. 'Ah, who will cure you of this
terrible selfishness?' it said sadly. Ahmad interrupted the
angel, 'Who or what are you? Are you good or evil?' The
angel replied, 'I am all goodness, I am your guardian angel
and protector.' It added, 'You will ignore my message at
your peril,' and then disappeared in a puff of smoke.
Finally Ahmad realised that he was awake and lay very still
thinking about his dream. Before dawn he resolved to
make the journey to Damascus in search of the sage and
his heart's desire.

The sultana and the seven princesses raised no protest
when Ahmad announced his departure. They were so
accustomed to his impetuous behaviour and spendthrift
ways that his story about an angel's message intrigued
them no more than any of his earlier lunatic schemes.
Ahmad left the palace on one of his fine steeds, with images
of the fun and adventures ahead swirling in his brain.
During the long, uneventful journey he tried to define the
substance of his heart's desire. He thought of all the things
that money could buy and realised that he did not really
want any of those things; besides, he already had more
costly possessions and extravagant purchases than he could
count.

Ahmad arrived in the great city of Damascus and rested
in a coffee house convinced that Ramadan the sage would
reveal everything to him. Ahmad visitied many coffee
houses before anyone admitted knowledge of an old man
called Ramadan. Finally (when he asked politely) someone told him where the old sage lived. The young sultan
pushed his way through the busy streets and alleyways of
the poor quarter of the city to Ramadan's house. The old

sage was waiting for him. 'Welcome young man, son of the great sultan. Enter O son of the most auspicious sultan. It is because of your noble father's name that you are welcome in my humble home.' Ahmad was startled by this ambiguous greeting but returned the customary thanks and expected responses.

The old man was ancient. He looked like he had been wandering the earth for more than one hundred years. His weak eyes squinted and watered as he peered at Ahmad. 'You have your good father's face, my boy,' he said, 'but I fear that the heart is not so similar.' Ahmad ignored this insult, not out of politeness, but because he rarely noticed unflattering comments. His mind set on discovering the meaning of the angel's visit, he interrupted the old sage, saying, 'I dreamed of an angel who told me to come here so that you would help me find my heart's desire. What is it, old man?' Ramadan the ancient sage said nothing for a moment, then he explained, 'You have misunderstood the angel's message, son of the great sultan. To find your heart's desire you must first know what it is.' Ahmad was annoyed and felt tricked; he wondered if Ramadan was just an old fool in his dotage and made as if to leave. The old man stopped him with a single gesture of one frail hand. 'Leave at your peril,' he warned in an unexpectedly fierce voice. 'Sit down, you young idiot, and listen to what I have to say.' For the first time in his entire life Ahmad felt the sharp sting of rebuke and was silent. He settled down on a cushion at the old man's feet. Ramadan asked, 'Do you have anything to say before I begin?' Ahmad answered, 'Please tell me why I had to come here, I have never been so curious about anything before. Why was I able to find you in the great city? It seemed as if fate guided me every step of the way.'

Ramadan began a long tale full of mystery and promise and revealed the following things which were to shape Ahmad's future: 'When you were born, son of the great sultan, a prophesy was made by the Seven Good Jinn who

served and protected your dear father. The Seven Jinn
were sent to your father because of his friendship with
King Suliman, Son of David, Lord of the Jinn and Master
of all Magicians, peace be upon him. And the prophesy?
The great Suliman once declared that a beautiful princess would be rescued from imprisonment by a young
sultan who would deliver the princess into his hands.'
Ahmad, impetuous again, forgot his manners and made
a sudden rude interruption. 'How do I come into this?'
he demanded, 'and what would I get out of bringing
some imprisoned girl to this King Suliman? What is the
prophesy concerning me, surely that's what I should
know!'

Ramadan gave Ahmad a disapproving look, 'Patience,
young man,' he warned, 'all will be revealed in time.'
Then the old sage continued his story: 'At your birth it
was prophesied that you would be the one to perform an
important task for King Suliman, peace be his forever. It
happens that the beautiful princess called Ayesha who has
been locked in a tower by her father can only be rescued
by a young handsome sultan. You should know that her
imprisonment is punishment for disobedience, she refused
to be King Suliman's wife and thus provoked her father's
wrath. You will rescue the Princess Ayesha and take her
to King Suliman, who will marry her. The task is yours
because it has been written into your fate. I am merely the
messenger and the giver of one gift which will help you in
your quest.'

The old sage reached into his robes and took out a small
looking glass rimmed with copper and silver. He gave
the mirror to Ahmad, saying: 'This is a magic mirror which
will help you on your way. You must look into it for
guidance on your quest to find the princess in the tower,
rescue her and then take her to King Suliman.' Ahmad was
thrilled by the prophesy which made him seem so important and heroic, and by mention of the powerful King
Suliman and the beautiful princess. 'What will happen

when I take this girl to King Suliman?' he asked. Ramadan replied, 'There is nothing that the Lord of the Jinn and Master of Magicians cannot do. If you succeed in your quest and rescue the princess and deliver her safely to Suliman's palace, you can claim any reward, you can even ask him for your heart's desire.' Ahmad left the old sage's house in high spirits, excited by the prospect of getting his heart's desire after all.

The young man set off on his quest. But soon, to his surprise, he found that he could not concentrate on the heroic adventures ahead. He was so troubled by images of the poor princess in the tower that he hardly thought of his own desires. When he thought of the Princess Ayesha he found himself admiring the resolve and courage with which she had opposed her father's wishes. The magic mirror showed him the route he had to take out of the city and before nightfall he came to the edge of the dark forest which hid the tall white tower where the princess was imprisoned. He looked into the mirror again and saw the image of a beautiful girl: it was the princess, frightened, tearful and alone in the tower. From time to time tiny tears ran from her eyes and the young man's heart was stirred. He fell in love with her in the vision and vowed to save her both from the tower and from the old king who wanted her for himself.

Ahmad drew his sword and began to cut a path through the thick undergrowth. He heard the sound of forest beasts all around and felt his rich robes being ripped to shreds by the sharp thorns of the bushes. But he did not falter or lose courage, and made a steady progress following the instructions which appeared in the magic mirror. At last, at midnight, he stood at the foot of a tall white tower which seemed to stretch up to heaven. There, high above him on the balcony, was the Princess Ayesha waiting patiently as if she had been waiting for him every night of her cruel confinement.

Ahmad did not hestitate, he called out: 'I am Ahmad the

sultan, son of the great sultan. I have come to rescue you.'
Ayesha nodded as if she had known that this would happen
one day. Ahmad took a ladder of silken rope from under
his robe and threw it high in the air to the princess. He
watched as she caught it with a deft, confident movement
and saw that she was even more beautiful in life than in
the vision in the mirror. 'Fasten the ladder securely and
climb down to me. I will catch you if you fall,' he said. The
princess nodded and did as he instructed, smiling with
delight that her dream had come true. Her sad imprisonment was over and she was escaping with this fine young
man's miraculous assistance. In a trice the princess had
climbed down the ladder and was in Ahmad's strong arms.
She smiled at him as if she had known him all her life.
'Thank you O sultan,' she said in straightforward delight.
As the starlight twinkled in their eyes they hoped that from
that moment on they could spend all of their days together.

Ahmad looked into the mirror again and saw old
Ramadan pointing to a path through the forest which led
to a magnificent palace far in the distance. This palace was
the home of King Suliman, Son of David. Ahmad realised
with a sinking heart that he had to go there and confront
the ancient and powerful king of all the magicians. The
rescue had been simple compared to the task ahead. Now
he had to find the courage to beg for the liberty of his
beloved princess so that she could be his wife. Ahmad took
Ayesha's hand and said: 'I cannot bear to part with you
dearest princess, I will marry you, but we must marry with
honour. First we must go to the palace and face the great
one, the powerful lord of all magical beings who controls
the Jinn.' Ahmad had realised that the visit to King
Suliman was a crucial part of his fate; if he shirked from
this ordeal the wrath of the king would follow him to the
ends of the earth and his magic would destroy him and his
love for Ayesha. The couple looked at each other, aware of
the danger ahead, and set off along the path resolved to
meet their fate.

The young sultan and the princess arrived at the enormous golden gates of King Suliman's palace and stopped. The magnificent palace looked deserted but suddenly, without warning, the gates swung open. The couple advanced to the great doors of the palace itself and they too opened as if by magic. Inside, despite their fear, they were enchanted by the beauty of the palace. There were chairs of pure gold encrusted with ivory and emeralds, the walls were of silver and covered with silken tapestries and a hundred mirrors. The palace sparkled like it was made of glass. The couple looked around the entrance chambers but it seemed quite empty. Ayesha sat down on a low couch and tried to stop trembling. Ahmad took her hand again and comforted her with soft words of love.

In the twinkling of an eye a great table appeared before them and invisible hands laid it with all manner of fine things to eat and drink. The rarest meats and fruits and aromatic wines tempted the couple and they began to satisfy their hunger, cautiously at first, then with increasing appetite until they felt almost at ease in this curious place. Enchanting music which seemed to flow out of the shining palace walls further soothed their fears. When they could eat and drink no more the table vanished as mysteriously as it had come.

Ayesha and Ahmad stared at each other, wondering what would happen next. A loud voice interrupted their thoughts: 'Welcome, young people, I trust you are pleased with my hospitality!' Ayesha's trembling intensified; this voice did not sound welcoming at all. Ahmad stood up and looked for the speaker, but he still could not see the human form of their powerful and dangerous host. 'Great King Suliman, Lord and Master of the Jinn, I have brought the Princess Ayesha to you as my fate has decreed,' Ahmad announced. 'But during my quest I have learned a great many things about life and I must discuss them with you. Will you appear in our humble presence?' He said these things with all the courage and nobility he could muster.

With a swirling of golden robes King Suliman swept into the centre of the room from behind one of the tapestries which concealed a secret passageway. He stood before Ahmad, a tall man with a commanding air and fierce green eyes which still burned with a dangerous fire despite his ancient age. He wore a white silk turban which shone like his long white beard, and the emerald pin which was set in the turban echoed the fire in his glittering eyes. His boots were of the finest leather and around his golden robes he wore a belt embroidered with silver stars. Caught in the old man's hypnotic gaze, the couple felt that he could read their deepest thoughts and they bowed low before him. King Suliman nodded to Ahmad as if encouraging him to speak, but poor Ahmad was tongue-tied with terror. 'Peace be upon you, great Suliman,' Ahmed stuttered at last. 'And upon you be peace,' the great lord responded. 'I am glad you have come here. I have been watching you in my magic opal, the gemstone I wear here on my ring,' Suliman explained, showing the couple the huge opal which half-covered his hand. Suliman paused for a moment, then he said, 'Well, you know what you know and you have something to tell me have you not?' His fierce green eyes seemed to gleam, but gave nothing away, while he held Ahmad in his fearful gaze.

Ahmad replied: 'I was honoured to carry out the task you had decreed because my father, God rest his soul, was a friend of yours, great Suliman. I was most honoured to rescue the Princess Ayesha,' his voice was shaking now, '. . . most honoured to do this task, but . . . but we have fallen in love and I beg you to let us marry.' The great Lord of the Jinn continued to stare at Ahmad, 'Do you often beg for things dear to your heart?' he asked. Ahmad started as if to reply, but remained silent, his eyes averted in deep shame. He realised that the great Lord Suliman, Master of the Jinn, knew everything about him, his extravagance, his wastefulness, his thoughtlessness and, particularly, the fact that until he met Ayesha he did not know his heart's desire. 'The princess is my heart's desire,' Ahmad said at last. 'I beg you to let us leave together in true knowledge of this, I beg you as I have never begged for anything before.'

Suliman watched and waited as if his silence was a mysterious ordeal which Ahmad would have to bear. Any foolish talk would destroy his chance of marrying the princess, yet if he did not speak, in the great lord's eyes the strength of his desire would seem diminished. 'I love the Princess Ayesha,' Ahmad said very simply. 'Ayesha is deeply sorry that she refused your offer of marriage but surely now she cannot refuse the demands of love from two hearts?'

'Brave and wise words, young sultan,' King Suliman said. The old man smiled, 'I see indeed that you have found your heart's desire. It is God's will, and let it be so. Remember that I knew this would happen because I know all things, and for the sake of your dear father I will bless your marriage to this beautiful creature. Go in peace and marry the Princess Ayesha with my blessing.' The happy couple thanked the Lord of the Jinn from the bottom of their hearts and prepared to leave the palace. Then Ahmad had a sudden thought. He paused and plucked up the courage to make one final request. 'There is one more favour I would ask you,' he began and King Suliman nodded. Ahmad continued: 'It is my heart's desire to be free of my spendthrift ways. I know this to be a great weakness and I must be cured. Is there a spell you could place on me to curb my extravagance?' The old man nodded again in approval and said: 'Young sultan, the spell you seek has already fallen over you. It is the spell of love. No spell of mine is more powerful than this and your weakness has gone forever as long as you love the Princess Ayesha.'

With these words King Suliman, Son of David, raised his arms and the silver room was plunged into darkness. The hundred flickering candles were blown out by a mighty wind and Ahmad and Ayesha felt themselves swept up into the heavens. They closed their eyes in terror and clutched each other so that they might not be blown apart by the magical whirlwind. When they opened their eyes again they were back in front of the gates of the great city of Damascus. The couple could not believe their luck. 'What miracles we have seen, beloved,' Ahmad said, 'was I dreaming or did they really happen?' Ayesha's eyes were shining with love. 'Ahmad, my love, it has been a day of miracles. First, you came to rescue me, then I fell in love with you and you with me, and finally King Suliman, Lord of the Jinn, allowed me to go with you. So how can all this be a dream since I am here beside you?' Ahmad laughed and held Ayesha tight in his arms. 'You are wise, my love, and the greatest miracle of all is that we will be married and my extravagance is cured forever.' Ayesha teased him, 'Time will tell, beloved Ahmad. Remember that the spell will last only as long as you love me.' Ahmad replied: 'Then it is as I said, I am cured forever!'

After many days Ahmad and the Princess Ayesha arrived back in Ahmad's own country and the sultana and his seven sisters all wept for joy at his safe return from the quest. When the sultana saw Ayesha she realised that her son's love for this beautiful girl had made him a man worthy of his father's reputation. Ahmad and Ayesha told their story to the sultana and preparations for the wedding started immediately. Meantime the Chief Treasurer came to Ahmad and announced that a camel train carrying gold had arrived at the palace. The palace coffers were brimming over with the gold, and if handled with care it was more than enough to last Ahmad and his family all their lives. Ahmad was mystified. 'Where did this come from?' he asked. The Treasurer handed him a scroll bound with an emerald green ribbon. Ahmad read: 'The treasury of the late sultan has been replenished by order of King Suliman, Son of David, Lord of the Jinn. Do not waste this gift, young sultan, and remember your heart's desire.'

Ahmad saw that the scroll was sealed with red wax imprinted with Suliman's seal, known as the luckiest of all good charms throughout Arabia.

Ayesha sent a letter to her father inviting him to the wedding and apologising for her past disobedience. The following day she received a reply in which he asked for her forgiveness and explained that imprisoning her had been the only way that he could avoid offending King Suliman. He blessed the impending marriage and declared that nothing would please him more than attending the wedding.

On the eve of the ceremony Ayesha went to Ahmad with a curious request. She announced that she could not marry him after all. She had nothing suitable to wear, she said, her robes were too shabby and unfit for her future role as a sultan's wife. Ahmad felt a sudden natural rush of anger in his veins. 'You have too many robes of excellent quality already. I'm not going to buy you a new robe until you really need it!' Ayesha burst into laughter. She laughed and laughed until she was weeping and Ahmad joined her as he realised that she had been testing him. The couple hugged each other in delight in the knowledge that Ahmad's extravagance had indeed disappeared.

It was a beautiful wedding and the joyous sounds of celebration echoed throughout the land. During the wedding feast the couple sat at the head of a great table which groaned under the weight of all the food. The sultana and Ahmad's sisters sat at one side, and Ayesha's wise father on the other. As the old man pronounced his joy at the wedding, a flock of white doves appeared in the sky. They flew into the banquet hall and dropped rose petals as they swooped low over Ahmad and Ayesha. Everyone wondered where the doves had come from, but the couple knew that this was a sign from King Suliman, Master of Magicians: the doves were his messengers bringing wedding congratulations.

Sultan Ahmad used his treasures for the good of his

people and in time he became as well loved as his father. The love he had found on his quest never deserted him, nor did he waste a penny of his riches. Ahmad remained a wise, kind and generous man throughout his life and God blessed the couple with many sons.

OUM SHERIF: A HOPELESS WOMAN

Oum Sherif always rushes into the room where the women meet as if pursued by wild dogs. She looks around fearfully, pants for breath and takes several minutes to relax after her dash through the streets. She brings her baby daughter and grips her so tightly during a tale that the child sometimes whimpers with discomfort. At the end of the evening, especially after one of the comic tales which Oum Sherif loves, she leaves the company seeming relaxed and happy, but the next evening she reappears as nervous and anxious as ever. Oum Sherif's life story throws light on these strange and often puzzling sides of her character.

I was born in a small village in the Western Desert about twenty-five years ago. I grew up there with my sisters and brothers, we were a family of ten children and my father's mother lived with us. My childhood was spent looking after our animals with the other girls. We would go off early in the morning and have nothing to do except make sure that nothing happened to the goats. It was very nice.

Some days I would stay at home with my mother and grandmother to help them with their work. I was given all sorts of tasks, mostly things like fetching and carrying or taking food to the men at work outside. I enjoyed that too. Life was simple and you always knew what would happen next. When it was one time of year we did a certain type of work, at another time of year there were different tasks. People all worked together and helped each other with big jobs like digging a well or repairing a wall. I can't explain what it was really like to be a child in a village, it's hard to imagine how you felt when you were a child, but I remember that it was a warm, friendly place. I remember lots of happy occasions and I remember the different times of year and the village feast days and celebrations best of all.

I was the youngest girl of the family, the third youngest of all the children. My baby brothers were fun and I liked to play with them, especially to tell them stories at night. When I became older I spent most of my time looking after them because my mother was not well. My sisters were all married when mother fell ill and so I had to do most of the housework too, but I enjoyed running a home by myself. My mother said it was good practice for the future when I would have a husband and a home of my own. It makes me very sad to think back to those days because I miss them very much. I wish I could go back in time and be a young girl playing at being a housewife again. It was easy then, whereas now I often feel that I can't cope with life here.

I was married in the village when I was sixteen and this was a big time of celebration for our family. My father and his brother arranged things between them and they had agreed a long time before, when I was just a child, that there would be a marriage between their youngest children. This is the usual way of things in the countryside and people know that it makes a good, secure marriage. One important thing is that the husband and wife usually know each other well because they are close relatives. Of course it's difficult to arrange to marry relatives in the city because people don't have many of their own kin living close by, but people still talk about it and try to arrange this kind of marriage whenever possible.

The problem with my marriage was that my father's brother had left our village when I was a child and moved away to another place. They were not able to visit very often, although my father and uncle kept in touch and stuck to their agreement. We are a very close family and are tied to one another by many marriages between cousins, but although the children of my generation were close in terms of blood and loyalty, we were not close or friendly as people.

When my husband came to meet me before the wedding I was as scared as if he had been a stranger. We didn't know each other at all and I didn't recognise him from childhood memories. I could tell that I was a stranger to him as well. It was a very strange meeting. The two of us felt embarrassed and were very cold to each other, while the rest of the family was busy celebrating their reunion. There was a great feast which lasted two days and nights. My sisters and their families all came burdened down with good things to eat, and my aunts and cousins and I had been cooking for days in advance. I knew that I should have been full of joy and excitement as a new bride-to-be, but there was a miserable ache in the bottom of my stomach which made me nervous and unhappy.

On the evening before my wedding my mother, still weak and unwell, and her sisters advised me about marriage. They told me things about married life as they oiled my hair and prepared me for my husband. They talked about pregnancy and sex and what a man expected of a wife. I was shocked by some of the things they said. They told me not to be too frightened but it was good if a bride was a little scared of what lay ahead. They said that a man expected his wife to weep and call for her mother on her wedding night. They said that a bride who acted normally would probably be divorced straight away because her husband would think that she'd been to bed with other men. Well, my wedding night came and went and it was not as terrible as I had feared. My mother and aunts were there to comfort me at the beginning. I was scared of course, but not hysterical, which is always a disaster. Gamal did all the things I had been told to expect and didn't seem displeased with my behaviour. I wept and bled as expected and the proof was there for all to see, so the wedding party continued and everyone was delighted.* I remember thinking how strange life had become. I was the wife of a

* The proof of virginity ceremony Oum Sherif refers to is called Doxla. In typical form it involves the bridegroom breaking the woman's hymen with a forefinger wrapped in a strip of gauze or cotton cloth. This takes place during the wedding feast in the presence of the bride's close female kin. Guests at the feast usually wait outside the bedroom door until the triumphant bride's kin and the groom appear and offer the blood-stained cloth for inspection. The·

man I didn't know, yet everyone acted as if we were old friends. I couldn't think of anything to say to him and he was cold and distant when we were together in public, which is correct, but also in private, even when we shared a bed.

My uncle and aunt, Gamal's parents, were very nice to me at first. They made me think that everything was fine. What they didn't tell me until the wedding celebrations were over was that Gamal was taking me to the city. First of all we moved to Gamal's village, just the four of us, Gamal and his parents and me. All I can remember about that trip was failing to hold back my tears and Gamal's mother scolding me for crying like a baby. The village was a long way from my mother and father and my baby brothers and I felt abandoned and alone. Gamal was very tough with me and told me off for a hundred things that I did wrong. I made a mess of the first meal I had to prepare and his mother was angry with me too. I didn't begin my married life with much success at all. But I was determined to try harder the next day and become a good wife. I didn't want to embarrass my parents by behaving badly, especially my mother who had taught me how to run a kitchen. If I made another mess people would say that she had taught me nothing.

This was the start of my battle against failure. Since then I've always tried as hard as I possibly can but it never seems good enough. However, there were no more major accidents while we stayed with my in-laws, but then Gamal and I didn't stay there for long. Before a full week had passed Gamal announced that we would leave for the city at dawn on the following day. With hardly any warning I

---

cloth is often ceremonially passed around before the festivities start up again. The bride and groom may return to join the party at this stage before the marriage is fully consummated. This is said to be because people want to look for signs that the bride has wept during Doxla, which is taken as extra proof of the bride's ignorance of sexual activity.

had to pack his possessions and rearrange my own marriage gifts so that everything fitted into one trunk. That was all we had, one trunk of things with which to build a married life together. Still, I was hopeful that it would be enough to sustain us until things improved.

I can see now that I hoped for too much, even my vague hope that we would reach some sort of understanding as husband and wife was foolish. Gamal and I started out as strangers despite our common blood and we never got any closer. Maybe this is because we both knew that we should be very close, but were ashamed because we didn't know how to make it happen. That seems like a very long time ago, although less than three years have passed, and now I believe that we are further apart than ever.

We set off for the city on foot with the trunk strapped to a donkey, a gift from my mother's brother. I used to hug that silly animal when Gamal was asleep since it had come from my mother's kin and this fact gave me some comfort. I don't think Gamal and I exchanged more than a few words during the day and at night he would lie beside me and say nothing at all. I prepared food when we stopped for the night and tried to cook special things to please him, but they never turned out well because I wasn't used to cooking over a camp fire. Gamal didn't scold me or complain but I sensed he wasn't pleased with how I was turning out. Although I was very frightened by the idea of the city, as I had never even been away from my parent's village before, I hoped that things would be better once our journey was over.

We were both very tired throughout the journey and my feet had been bleeding quite badly, but I tried to keep that hidden from Gamal in case he became angry and thought I was weak. Every morning when we set off again I hoped that we would soon be settling into a new life in our marital home and learning to become friends. Like most of the things I used to hope for, that didn't happen and I've given up hope now. Since we came to the city I've grown more and more hopeless. That's the truth of it, I'm ashamed to say!

Gamal and I finally reached a town outside the city, although in my ignorance I thought it was Cairo itself. I was really scared when I saw the crowds of people and the traffic. I was sure that there was a madman somewhere in the crowd who was about to rush out and kill us. It was so noisy that my mind went blank. I couldn't hear Gamal when he told me that we were going to travel the rest of the way by bus. I had never been on a bus and I had never sat with a crowd of strangers before, so I didn't cope very well when he pushed me on board. Everything was suddenly new and unknown. I had no idea what to do so I just screamed and cried and called for my mother. He was very angry with me then and I don't think he will ever forgive me for the fuss I made that day. Of course I behaved very badly and I'm ashamed to think of it now, but at that time I was still a child in many ways and perhaps he could have been less harsh with me.

In any case Gamal didn't speak to me again during the journey and when we arrived in Cairo very late that night he behaved as if I was invisible. I was really scared by the thought that he was trying to lose me. It wouldn't have been difficult, because I was so nervous and the city was enormous. But I stuck close to him, determined not to let him abandon me in this frightening place. Although it was very late there were hundreds of people around, everywhere you looked there were people. I hadn't known that there were so many people in the world, but here they were packed into a few streets.

Gamal went to find his friend, who offered us a space to sleep. This man and his wife were friendly and kind to us, but I was too scared to make much of an impression. This made me feel even worse since I wanted his friends to like me. The next morning Gamal shook me awake, I had overslept and he was really angry with me again. I excused myself to the woman of the house. She didn't seem to mind and told me not to apologise, but I knew Gamal was furious and thought me lazy and rude.

After breakfast Gamal's friend took us to a place where we could set up house. It was not far from where his rooms were, although it looked more derelict. There were a lot of people working, all crowded together on a piece of ground among the tents, huts and tombs. I could hardly believe it when I heard Gamal's friend say that they were all building homes. Some men came to ask questions and I hid behind Gamal. I knew that people were looking at me and laughing and I felt stupid, but I didn't know how to behave.

The men started to collect materials which could be used to make a rough dwelling and I did whatever they asked and carried and fetched things I could manage to lift. After a while Gamal gave me some money and told me to find the market and buy food. We had some tea and basic supplies left but no bread or stuff like that. I remember wandering around lost and in a daze, too timid to ask a stranger for directions. That was when I met Oum Mohammed and Amira for the first time and I'll never forget how kind they were.

I had been lost for ages although I really wasn't far from where Gamal was working, I'd just been walking in a big circle. I remember fighting with my tears and failing again, then sitting down on a wall and sobbing. I didn't know that this was Amira's wall and when this woman suddenly touched my arm I jumped so much that I fell over. She introduced herself, helped me inside and made me tea. It had been a very long time since I'd heard a kind voice and she reminded me of my mother. It was as if I had fallen under her spell of kindness. I remember that I poured my heart out to Amira and told her all about myself. A visitor arrived soon after I had dried my tears and this was my first meeting with Oum Mohammed. Those two women saved me that day. They gave me water to try to clean up a bit and then took me to the market.

I had hurt my leg when I fell off the wall and was limping, though trying not to. Oum Mohammed noticed and she ordered me to sit down and wait while she bought the groceries. I was shocked by the way that all the women behaved in the market in the presence of men. There was a great deal of shouting, some women even yelled at the men who were selling things. There were so many strange new sights and experiences in those first days in the city.

When the groceries were bought, Oum Mohammed announced that she wanted to meet my husband. This surprised me most of all, but then I had only just met Oum Mohammed myself and knew nothing of her courage. The fact that a woman, even an old and wise one, could initiate a meeting with a man was also new to me. But I was so overwhelmed by affairs that I described where I thought my husband was and let myself be led back to him.

I still don't know if Gamal was pleased or angry with me when I returned with a big bag of groceries and a talkative old woman. He was very polite and friendly and I was happy to see him like this for the first time. Everyone chatted and discussed things with Oum Mohammed while I made tea and prepared a light meal. Gamal's friend knew Oum Mohammed and they were soon reminding each other of useful things to tell us about the neighbourhood. Gamal didn't even look cross when Oum Mohammed told him that I had hurt my leg and advised him not to be too hard on me because I was still a child. I was very happy and I still remember my first night in this neighbourhood with pleasure.

Gamal and I fixed up a roof and walls in a few days and built ourselves a home. We still live in the same place, although there have been some additions since then. Gamal found a job in another district with the help of his friend and went off to work there every day. These few things are all I can remember about the early days here. Nothing changed between us until I became pregnant, when he showed a lot of affection and concern. I was very ill then but I tried to pretend that I was fine and this caused all sorts of extra problems. Amira was very kind during my pregnancy. She spent a lot of time and went to a lot of trouble looking after the house for me when Gamal was out.

Gamal doesn't like me making friends and he is always criticising other women's behaviour in the city. He doesn't understand that women here have no time to worry about modest ways of life when they're busy trying to stay alive. Gamal tells me not to go out and so I try not to disobey him, but he's away from the area from dawn to dusk so he can't be sure whether I obey him or not. Still, I don't want to disobey him and I always followed his every command when we first arrived. At that time I depended on visitors for company and there were some women who came often and we became friends. I'll always be grateful for their kindness when I was ill and pregnant. I don't think I would have survived my grief after the death of my son without their comfort and support.

Sherif died when he was two months old and I'll never recover from this as long as I live. I have another baby now, she's just five months old and I thank God that she seems healthy. But the memory of Sherif is always with me. No mother who loses a son ever fully recovers from his death. I feel that Sherif had no chance of life in this place. We were too poor and lived in too much dirt for a baby to survive. Gamal and I were both working when he died, trying to make enough money to feed ourselves but never making enough. I was so hungry that I had no milk and despite all my efforts to cure this I ended up starving my son to death. I can't bear to think about this and won't say anything else about Sherif, except that I'll never forget him or stop mourning for him. Now my life is lived for Fatima, my baby daughter.

Gamal is an unpleasant stranger who sometimes shares my bed but he has nothing to do with any other part of my life. I have come to accept that our marriage is unhappy and that Gamal is probably as unhappy as I am. We live in an unhappy silence together, he never talks to me. He didn't try to comfort me after Sherif died, instead he spent his time with the men in the coffee house and shared his grief with them. I know he blames me for Sherif's death, and the loss of a son must be the greatest crime a woman can commit. My greatest fear is that he might divorce me someday and that would be unbearable. I can't imagine how I would cope alone and look after Fatima.

My family are so far away that I could never get a message to them. I have no money to return to them either, although if I came into a fortune I would go back to them tomorrow. I grieve for them as if they're already dead. Perhaps they are, I wouldn't know. If Gamal divorced me I don't think that I could find a job which pays well enough to look after Fatima properly. You see, you have to know someone in the workshop who can arrange for you to get this kind of job and I've never met anyone who works away from home. Perhaps I should go out more often despite Gamal's warnings and try to make more friends. But when I start to think about this kind of thing and imagine being divorced, each different solution seems equally hopeless.

However, I'm still a young woman and I have a lovely daughter. I must never forget this and I try to cope as best I can. I try to make the best of life and not give in to tears of despair and self-pity. Of all the dangers in the world self-pity must be the worst. Gamal may not like me, or care for me, or bother to talk to me, but he provides what food he can and he cares for Fatima. He knows I try my best and sometimes he's not too harsh with me. He came home early once and found the table untidy because I was working at my sewing job. He said nothing and wasn't angry, because he knows that I work hard to earn money and of course he feels uncomfortable about that. His life hasn't been easy since he left the village either.

At the moment I have to confess that I've given up hope that things will get better. I can't imagine anything which would change my relationship with Gamal, apart from a miracle. Certainly we would need a miracle to put an end to our everyday struggle against hunger and hardship, and nothing will ever bring back Sherif. Still, I know from my friends that I'm not alone with my problems. There are many women here who suffer from hunger and bad husbands and even the death of their dearest sons. It makes me sad to think of them, and I wish all our lives could be different. If I could learn how to make life a little easier for us all I would be the happiest woman alive. But perhaps I will find some wisdom and strength to work on this impossible task when I grow older.

Oum Sherif fed her baby while the tea cups were filled for the second time that evening. The baby nuzzled and grunted with such satisfaction that she drew admiring comments from several of the women. Oum Sherif moved across to the more crowded corner of the room beside the other young mothers with babies. Although as a relative newcomer she was shy at making the first move to join them, the women soon were swapping details of recent childbirth experiences. They were interrupted by the call for a tale and the storyteller's response.

THE SEVENTH CHANCE

This is a tale about hope in the face of despair and the need to look beyond the horizon. In this tale a fine young woman is doomed unless help is found in the most unlikely of places.

Once there was a lovely young girl who adored her parents. She lived in order to please them and was the kindest daughter imaginable. The fact that they all lived in a castle and that her father was a king, her mother a queen, and the girl herself a fine princess doesn't matter at all. She was a lovely girl and deserved the very best the world could offer, although her position seemed to ensure that she would not be short-changed. It only mattered that she was a princess to a gang of wicked bandits. It was well known that the princess loved her father and he loved her more than all the treasures in his kingdom. This was enough for the bandits and they devised a wicked plan.

One day the princess was out strolling in the castle gardens when she heard a soft cry coming from the bushes. It sounded like a baby and because she was a brave and tender-hearted girl she was determined to investigate. The princess crawled into the bushes only to find three evil-looking men who seized her, tied her up and carried her off. These bandits were not the foolish half-wits who appear in other tales, but clever and cunning. They had dug a deep tunnel under the castle wall, which came out in the middle of the bushes. Having accomplished their evil deed, they carried the princess out through the tunnel and escaped unseen to their desert hide-out.

The king and queen were horrified and mystified by their daughter's disappearance. It was only when a ransom note arrived demanding all the king's wealth in exchange for the princess that they realised she had been captured by bandits.

Meantime the brave princess was trying her best to fight against the bandits. Every time one came near enough she would bite him as hard as she could. She got slapped for her efforts but didn't mind at all. The recollection of the pain and outrage on the bandit's face helped to soothe her stinging cheek. The princess kicked and punched and bit the bandits whenever she had an opportunity. This was not very ladylike behaviour, but she thought that it was the right thing to do in such circumstances. If the poor king and queen had been able to see her they would have agreed wholeheartedly. But the princess struggled in vain. After every small victory over the bandits they just tied her up tighter and beat her harder. Eventually she decided not to exhaust herself further with useless protests but to watch and wait for the first chance of escape from her captors.

The princess watched and waited for three days. On the evening of the third day the bandits grew careless.

They had been celebrating their success and the receipt of a message from the king, who had announced that they could have whatever they wanted if they released his daughter unharmed. The princess was furious, not because her father was willing to give up everything for her, but because these wicked men were managing to cheat a great man so easily! The bandits got very drunk and started to sing. The princess covered her ears because these were vulgar bandits' songs with lyrics which shocked her innocent ears. But she was becoming less innocent by the minute. The bandits got more and more drunk and grew yet more careless. One of them fell over right beside the princess and was soon snoring, quite unconscious with alcohol.

The princess knew an opportunity when she saw one. She wriggled slowly and painfully until she was at his side. She ignored the ropes which cut into her soft arms and ankles. She twisted and turned until she was able to grip his dagger in her teeth, then she gently tugged until it was free of its sheath. The other men were still drinking and carousing, and didn't notice a thing. The princess waited and watched, and some hours later when all the men had collapsed in a snoring, farting heap, she started to stab at the ropes as best she could with the dagger. It took a long time and she cut herself quite badly whenever the dagger slipped from her teeth. But determined as she was, the ropes soon frayed and finally snapped. She was free. Without a second thought she ran off into the desert as fast and far away as her legs could carry her. At dawn she realised that she was lost and alone. All around as far as the eye could see there was nothing but barren rocky desert.

The princess was very tired and hungry and thirsty, because she had not had food, water or sleep for a whole day and night. But there was no sign of the bandits' camp. She grew more cheerful imagining their fury when they discovered her escape. With typical determination she plucked a scraggy root which had somehow survived in this barren place and chewed on it cautiously. It tasted awful, not a delicate morsel fit for a princess, but it was moist and would sustain her. She had greater problems to solve than finding a palace banquet in the desert! The princess chose a direction at random and started to walk. The sun grew higher and hotter, but she walked on and on. She often fainted, but recovered her strength and continued. She fell into deep gullies, down dunes and into the crevices which scarred the landscape, but each time she dragged herself out and moved on in the same hopeless fashion.

Day after day she somehow survived, living on the desert plants and roots which shared her perilous existence. At night she huddled against a rock for warmth and wept, not so much from self-pity as from exhaustion and desperation. She wept as much for her parents, who would be frantic with worry, as for herself. She was filled with fury when she thought of the bandits who had caused this terrible situation. But this fury gave her a kind of strength and despite her tears she would set off again before sunrise.

As time passed the princess began to learn about her surroundings and appreciate the toughness of the few plants and creatures which had adapted to the desert and survived. She experimented with different roots and could soon tell which ones were more juicy than others. She learned to walk through the night, despite the danger of predators, and to hide under rocks by day. There were near-fatal mistakes which she also learned from, like checking that a safe-looking cave was empty before she went inside. Once she had been confronted by an outraged wild cat which defended its lair with teeth and claws. She was lucky to escape alive. Her dress was torn to shreds but she suffered no more than a deep gash, although this would have split her in two had she not been as fast on her feet as the beast itself.

The princess lost track of time as she wandered on through the never-changing landscape. She started to walk towards the horizon, although it always looked the same: more rocks, more dunes and more emptiness. Each day she hoped that someone would suddenly appear and save her. At least once a day she thought that she saw a figure in the distance, but it was always just a cruel trick played by imagination and the blinding sun. The day came when at last she gave way to despair. The princess could find no glimmer of hope to give her the courage to go on. She sank under a rock and thought that she would die there. As she waited for vultures to rip into her flesh, she became aware of a strange sound. It was an impossible and unfamiliar splashing sound like a bird taking a bath. She opened her eyes, turning her head wearily, and there not far away was a cluster of thin trees set around a small pool. An oasis!

Indeed she had not been mad, because there were birds splashing in the pool, delighting in the water which washed the desert dust from their feathers. The princess cursed herself for her weakness and forgot her previous despair as she ran to the pool. An oasis meant that people would come, and people meant that at last she would be rescued.

The princess drank and washed in the small pool and delighted in the water as much as the birds. These birds sat together on the same branch and watched her curiously, but the princess did not take much notice of them. She explored the oasis, just a few trees and the pool, but it was enough to sustain life and she saw the remains of a camp fire. She was shaking with excitement at this discovery. If nomads had been here recently they would return. She did not pause to think that nomads are nomads because they move from one place to another, they don't often leave one place and then return straight away. But she was dizzy with hope and so spent each day under a tree watching and waiting for the nomads to come back.

The birds sat in the tree above the princess but she ignored them. There were seven birds in all. If the princess had taken an interest she would have identified them easily. There was a sandgrouse, a raven, a buzzard, a

vulture, a kite, a babbler and, finally, a hoopoe. If she had
given them a second glance she would have thought that
they were a curious bunch of companions, not known for
their sociability and rarely seen together in a desert, on the
same branch of the same tree. Indeed it was rarer still for
such birds to display a great interest in lost princesses. If
the princess had been less intent on watching the horizon
for her nomad rescuers she would have noticed their antics
and profited from their wisdom.

First the sandgrouse flapped its wings and swooped
down beside the princess. It flew from side to side in front
of her. The bird soared as high as it could towards the
burning sun then dived dramatically, trying to attract her
attention. The little sandgrouse had a sad and soulful
nature. It lived to devote itself to romantic causes like
unrequited love and saving lost princesses, but despite all
its efforts she did not notice the sandgrouse.*

The raven made the second attempt. It started to sing.
Now ravens are not renowned for their fine voices and of
course this was the raven's clever plan. But although it
croaked and cawed until it was hoarse the princess did not
hear a thing. This terrible noise shattered the desert silence
but the princess sat watching for the nomads who would
save her and she quite ignored the raven with the tuneless
song.

The third bird tried to catch the princess's eye. The
buzzard, famed for its powerful wings and skill in hunting
snakes, was determined not to be ignored. It put aside its
pride and with a sudden jerk threw itself off the branch.
The princess looked up in surprise as the bird fell at her
feet. The buzzard hopped around in a most undignified
manner, nodding its big head and blinking at the princess
with its big round eyes.† But she looked away, finding

*. The sandgrouse features in early Arab poetry and in many Egyptian folk
songs and stories as a symbol of lost love and yearning for love. It is also
appreciated for another quality: being good in the pot.
† There is a species of 'snake-eating' buzzard found only in the Sinai Desert

nothing significant in the buzzard's behaviour. In her eyes it was a just another stupid bird.

The fourth bird, the vulture, took over from the buzzard and landed right in front of the princess. It stood beside her, so close that anyone else would have taken fright. But the princess flapped her hands and shooed away the huge vulture as if it was a fussy hen. The princess was so still as she sat staring out into the desert that she might have been carved from stone. She was too lost in thought dreaming of her rescuers to care that a vulture was perching on her feet.

The kite came next to give the princess her fifth chance of rescue. He spread his beautiful black wings and soared high above her. He swooped down to an outcrop of rocks and picked up some pebbles, then flew above the oasis. One by one he dropped the pebbles, which fell around the princess like rain. The kite continued to do this for a very long time. Since the princess paid little heed to the first stones which fell from the sky, the bird should not have bothered a second, third or fourth time. The kite finally returned to the branch in frustration to join the other birds. So far they had all failed to make the princess aware that help might come from a less obvious source than unpredictable nomads.

The bird called the babbler made the sixth attempt. He gave an impression of being rather foolish with his dim-witted babbling, although in fact he was a very smart bird. The babbler had learned many clever things through his love of gossiping, particularly how to mimic other creatures. He did not move from the branch above the princess but opened his beak and made a noise like the screech

---

region of Egypt which fits this description. It is very owl-like in appearance with a large head distinguished by a disc of dark feathers. There is some speculation that this is the bird depicted in a hieroglyph first thought to represent some type of owl. The buzzard's almost exclusive diet of snakes would certainly have fascinated the ancient Egyptians, as did the similar diet of the mongoose.

of a hungry baby. He changed the screech into a louder piercing wail and the princess suddenly looked up. She was sure that there was a baby somewhere nearby, although she knew that this was a mad thought. The clever babbler suddenly stopped screeching and made no sound at all, which is a very unusual thing for a babbler to do. Instead he flew after the princess as she began to search for the baby. The babbler started to mimic a baby again and each time the princess turned in the direction of the noise. The princess was coming close to discovering what the babbler wanted. It might take some time but at least she was no longer staring uselessly at the empty horizon.

What the seven wise birds knew, and as yet the princess didn't, was that a camel train was passing by the oasis. The birds had been watching it for some days and trying to make the princess notice the clouds of sand and dust it raised in the distance. If the birds could only manage to get her to see the dust cloud it would lead her to the rescuers she sought. They knew that her hope of the nomads' return was a foolish distraction. The nomads would not come back this way for many months. The princess did not know much about other people's way of life. Of course she had no need to when she had lived in a castle. The princess thought that she had learned a lot so far, as indeed she had, but she was making a common mistake. The big mistake was to cling to one particular hope when in fact there were other less obvious solutions to her plight.

The princess was distressed because she could not find the baby. She told herself that she was insane. There could not be a baby in this desolate place, its cries were part of her madness. Then she told herself that there might be an abandoned child who had been sleeping until those stupid birds disturbed it. The birds watched in horror as the princess stumbled through the oasis and out into the desert itself. She did not care where she was going now because she was at her wits' end. The princess fell over a rock and cut her knee, then lay in the dust and wept. She had wasted her last store of strength trying to find an imaginary baby and she sobbed for the baby and herself. Every hope of rescue had gone. She did not want to live and would not try to get up. She heard the baby screech again, louder than ever, and covered her ears to shut out the sound. The babbler's clever plan had failed and he flew back to the branch feeling unusually sad.

The seven birds crowded together on the branch and discussed their next move. The princess had been given six chances of escape but remained ignorant of them. She had not understood that the birds were trying to show her the importance of looking beyond the horizon. The dust raised by the camel train was not visible unless you looked right at the point where the earth meets the sky. The princess had scanned every dune and rock and track, the obvious place to look for travellers, but she did not know how to use her eyes in the desert and read desert signs. It was vital to forget the obvious boundaries of her desert prison and look further.

The birds were her only means of escape. The problem was that she was sure that people would rescue her. Now this is the crux of the matter. Listen hard! Naturally *people* would rescue her, the men who would take her back to her father and mother were not birds! But the birds were her means of escape. They were offering her the chance of rescue and without them she would never find the people! The princess would have seven chances because there were seven birds. However, the seventh chance would also be the last chance. The seventh bird hesitated but it could not hesitate for long. This was the hoopoe, the most beloved and honoured of birds.* The hoopoe saw that the princess

---

* The hoopoe is said to be the 'most honoured of birds' because it is mentioned in the Holy Quran (Sura 27, 20–8). The Quranic story tells how a hoopoe acted as messenger between the prophet Sulayman or Suliman (Solomon) and the queen of Saba (Sheba) in a time of great struggle against sin and evil. In Arab folklore the hoopoe was rewarded for this service with the coronet of feathers which has crowned all hoopoes since that day.

was almost beyond help. It knew that she had given up hope of rescue but it also believed that it was not too late. The honoured bird had a special gift, a gift it could use to save her, but it could only use this gift at a great cost to himself.

A very long time ago when the world was young, a hoopoe had helped a mighty soldier fight a dangerous battle. When the battle was won the bird was rewarded with the gift of human speech.*

The hoopoe could speak and understand any human language, and although it never dared to use the gift of speech, it often listened. This explains why it is often seen near people: it is curious to hear what they say. The hoopoe did not want to waste its wonderful gift through idle chatter and it did not forget the warning which accompanied the gift. The warning was a harsh reminder of God's all-seeing, all-knowing power. It was said that when the bird spoke with its human tongue God would hear and know that the hoopoe had chosen to be a man.

The seven birds debated what this warning meant and could not agree. One said that the hoopoe would die on the spot. One said that it would turn into a man. One said that it would lose his wings. One said that it would never be able to speak or sing again. Each bird could only guess at the terrible outcome of the hoopoe daring to speak, and each one in turn wished it well with a heavy heart. The hoopoe did not know what would happen either, but it chose to defy the warning even if it meant death. It knew that the princess was dying now and it wanted to save her. It knew that she had hoped for human help and perhaps if it spoke in a human voice she could be saved.

The princess was lying where she had fallen in the dust

* I am not aware of any variations on the Quranic story in which the hoopoe received the gift of human speech as an additional reward, but numerous folk stories, as implied by the reference on p. 176, and many of the tales in this collection feature birds and beasts which have the ability to converse with humans as part of their magical power.

of the desert. Her eyes were closed and her breath came in little gasps. The hoopoe flew, perhaps for the last time, and perched on her shoulder. It opened its beak and in a firm gentle voice said: 'Princess, help is at hand.' The bird did not die instantly, that was not its fate.

The princess opened her eyes. She looked for a man but saw only a bird. She tried to make sense of things but was too weak to understand what was happening. She wanted to sleep forever.

The hoopoe cleared its throat and spoke for the second time: 'Princess, listen and wake up. Help is at hand, you can be rescued if only you get up.' This time the hoopoe was more insistent. The bird had not turned into a man, that was not its fate.

The princess tried to rouse herself. Where was this help? Where was this man who was telling her such impossible things? She wanted to believe the things she heard because her hope was returning. It was better to die with hope, she thought. The princess tried to stand up but fell to her knees. The hoopoe jumped from her shoulder and stood before her. It saw that she watched it intently. 'Are you a talking bird? Are you the one who says help is at hand?' she asked. The hoopoe nodded, then began to speak rapidly, suddenly fearful that it would lose its wings before the princess was saved: 'Come, follow me! There's a camel train nearby! Keep looking beyond the horizon, watch for the dust from the camel train!' The hoopoe swooped high in the sky ar.d hovered until it saw the princess stumbling after. It had not lost his wings, that was not its fate.

The princess followed the bird, leaving the oasis far behind. Her weak eyes searched for the cloud of dust churned by a camel train, the sign that she would be saved after all. The hoopoe's keen eyes could see it quite clearly, but would the princess be able to distinguish that faint blur beyond the horizon?

The hoopoe hovered above the princess and urged her to see. Then it perched on her shoulder and pressed its beak against her cheek, nudging her head in the right direction so that she might notice the dust of the approaching caravan. The bird was stricken with fear that it would be punished before it led her to safety. But it saw that the camel train was coming closer. The minutes seemed like hours until at last the hoopoe soared into the air and cried out: 'Princess call to them, call to them!'

And so this is how the princess was saved. She called for help, and the drivers heard and came to the rescue. She was so weak that the sight of these tall, strong men made her fall into a faint. She did not know that the men recognised her straight away because the king had sent word of his daughter's capture throughout the kingdom. The princess was in such a deep faint that she did not stir when the men lifted her into their caravan, or when their boy servant gently wet her lips with water and honey. But none of this mattered a bit because of course she was safe at last. The camel train had travelled many miles before the princess recovered her senses. She was still too weak to speak, but now she knew that she was safe and on her way home.

The princess listened while the camel drivers' boy servant told the story of her rescue. He told of the caravan's long journey through the desert and their first sight of the princess. Then the boy told of the hoopoe, the bird which had seemed to call them to help the princess. Even simple children know things that are mysteries to fine princesses, so when the boy told another story about the hoopoe and his gift of speech the princess was amazed [see p. 174]. She remembered the lovely, gentle voice and the comforting tone and the wise words which brought about her rescue.

Despite her relief at being safe, despite her great joy at returning to her parents, the princess was deeply troubled. She was anxious about the bird, had it really perished in order to save her? What about the warning never to use its gift of human speech? She asked the boy how the hoopoe would suffer for saving her. The boy repeated the story:

'Some say that it dies at once, others say that it turns into a man, some say that it loses its wings, and still others that it will never utter another sound.' The princess searched her memory for some clue. What had been the hoopoe's fate? She remembered that the bird had not died, and it had not become a man, and it had not lost its wings. Finally, she wondered if the bird's punishment was that it would never utter another sound. The princess asked the boy: 'Would it be a dreadful punishment for a bird never to utter another sound?' The little boy thought for a moment, then replied: 'Perhaps birds are too happy to sing in Paradise.'

The princess arrived back at the castle fully recovered from her ordeal and the king and queen held a great party which lasted for more than a week. The camel drivers received a great reward for their kindness and news reached the palace that the bandits had killed each other in a terrible brawl. Everyone in the kingdom rejoiced at the safe return of the princess. Of course she was happier than she had ever been before and knew that she was the luckiest girl in the world. From that day forth she never forgot to feed the birds in the castle gardens and she never forgot that hope is the finest virtue.

Fatima whimpered at her mother's squeezes more frequently that evening. Oum Sherif had the baby bound in a tight shawl and this must have added to her discomfort on a very hot night. Everyone was delighted by the tale; its jokes and double-meanings had amused us, and there was enough adventure and romance to please the most seasoned critic. The women agreed that the princess was the ideal heroine; she was plucky and clever but not too perfect. The women delight in casting aspersions on any flawless character who seems too good to be true, whether in a tale or real life.

There was a lengthy discussion of the tale, fuelled by more tea and cakes, although Oum Sherif took no part in this. She had excused herself when the tale was over, saying that she had to leave in case her husband returned from the coffee house and discovered her absence. There was a louder than usual series of requests to stay on and protests at her early departure. Oum Idris muttered a thinly disguised curse on Gamal for the unreasonable demands he made on his young wife. None of this changed Oum Sherif's mind and delayed her departure, but she was clearly touched by the demonstration of friendship. Soon after Oum Sherif left the room it was remarked that she had been very happy that particular evening and seemed to be learning how to relax with her friends.

OUM MUSTAFA: A MANLESS WOMAN

The most prosperous woman in the group, Oum Mustafa, is a popular hostess. Her cakes are the most expensive on offer and her well furnished room is the most comfortable place to meet. Oum Mustafa sometimes seems boastful, although this is probably unintentional since she is careful not to offend the other hostesses. She is especially concerned about appearing to challenge Oum Mohammed's outright supremacy as *grande dame* of the storytelling circle. Oum Mustafa likes to sit on a stool in the middle of the gathering and she can see everything from this vantage point although it is a much lower stool than Oum Mohammed's. Oum Mustafa is a renowned storyteller, although she never offers a tale and always reminds the company of Oum Mohammed's superior skill whenever someone makes a direct request. However, she tells an excellent tale whenever there is an adequate degree of persuasion. Oum Mustafa enjoys talking about herself, particularly about the past, in the company of friends and neighbours. Like all good storytellers she elaborates on her favourite themes and expects equally elaborate praise from her audience. After a protracted long-winded courtship Oum Mustafa finally granted my request to record her life story. She talked about her life with a frankness I had not expected, and as the life story reveals, her public persona is a relatively recent creation.

I have always lived in this neighbourhood, and that's forty-two years now. But during married life, with a husband to care for and the children to raise, I didn't know much about other people's everyday life. Now that I'm busy running the stall it's a very different world, you can't fail to get involved in the activity and affairs of the street.

This past year since my husband's death I've seen people come and go, learned the names of market traders, met vendors in the square and discovered local short-cuts and back alleyways. I've found out all sorts of things about the neighbourhood that I didn't know before. Maybe this doesn't sound very important, but it's very important to me. It's the one thing that must be mentioned in the story of my life. I have had two lives, you might say, one during my marriage and one after it.

During the twenty-eight years that I was married I rarely left my husband's house. He provided me with everything I needed. I was completely safe and secure inside the house and never had to face the hubbub of the streets. It was a pleasant life and I'm proud that I lived this way. When I was Yussef's wife my life was always calm and easy because I never had to go out in public.

Yussef made sure that I had everything I needed to look after the house and he was always generous. He brought our food home and chose my clothes and everything like that. It was wonderful not having to work, although I didn't know that then. I was never lonely because I was always busy looking after the house and there were lots of visitors. My husband liked to invite his friends home so they could see what a good wife he had. I enjoyed preparing food for them, knowing that my Yussef was proud of my domestic skills. My friends also came to see me at home and when you returned their visits it was a matter of a quick walk to their house and then inside. You would never think of meeting outside, or enjoying the time you spent in the noisy, busy streets. The world outside was dangerous, that's how I thought of it then and in many ways I still do, even though my life has had to change so much.

Since Yussef's death I've had to learn many things about that world which would cause him much shame. His death was so sudden and the cause of so much grief and hardship that I will never recover from it. But God's ways are always for the good, even if people can't understand them at the time. The fact that I've had to provide for myself since Yussef's death by running his stall has caused me much grief. But this work has also given me a chance to learn about life outside and it's opened me to new experiences. I think I am a better person because I have had to go through this hardship. For one thing, work in the streets has taught me that many women don't have the easy life I took for granted when I was married to a devoted, hard-working man. I've seen a lot of things I'd rather not have seen and I've learned what it's like to feel shame, guilt and embarrassment without a man to protect you. I am a stronger woman because of all this and that is God's will.

I make my money selling fruit and some vegetables from the stall my husband used to run. I depend on the help of my two sons, who are my pride and joy. They give me the strength to struggle on. It was difficult to know what to do when Yussef died. I was a widow with two young sons to support and, what's worse, I was completely ignorant about money and terribly afraid. But I've survived, although sometimes that fact surprises me and it hasn't been easy. Thank God that my daughters were married to decent men before Yussef was taken from us; I could never have provided for their weddings at that time myself. I was quite hopeless in those days.

I've made many mistakes over the years, especially when I first tried to run the stall, but the other vendors were always kind and generous. As well as the usual pity for a widow, I'm sure they were sorry for me because I didn't have a clue how to look after myself. Perhaps at the time they were more patient with me than I deserved, because I was full of self-pity and despair. I behaved as if I was the only widow in the world who had to start providing for herself and family. Back in those terrible days after Yussef's death I was totally helpless.

Yussef died suddenly after just two days of fever. The doctors I sent for said that he died of a 'serious illness', although I'm sure it was their bad medicine which killed him.* Yussef was such a strong, healthy man that a fever

---

* Most people depend on the advice and drugs of pharmacists since few can afford doctors' fees. Free health care exists but local people have a low opinion

would not have killed him so quickly without any warning. I mourned without any sense of consolation for three months. Throughout this time I just sat weeping and wailing for my dead husband. I didn't sleep or wash or brush my hair and had hardly eaten since his funeral. I was on the brink of madness when my sister was sent for. She came at once and brought me back to sanity.

First she collected the children, who were with my neighbours: imagine that I'd even forgotten my sons in my grief! Then she set to work on my grief and fear and forced me to face life again. At that time my sister had her own worries. She had just been divorced by a man who hadn't cared either for her or for his duties as a husband. She knew what a good husband Yussef had been, but still she made me come to terms with the fact of his death and get my life and home back into proper order. With God's help and her urging, my strength and hope for the future were gradually restored. My sister had to work to keep food in her husband's house, so she knew all about money and coping with public life whereas of course I knew nothing about anything like that. She contacted Yussef's suppliers in the big market and got a neighbour to send a message to our father's cousins in the countryside. She organised everything so that I would be able to start up Yussef's business again. Then she told me about her plans.

Well, I had always considered myself to be a calm, even-tempered woman, but when I heard about the new way of life my sister had been arranging for me I lost my temper. My grief and pride mixed together and poured out in a

---

of doctors who do not charge fees. They argue that the free doctors must be badly trained, otherwise they would become private, expensive doctors. An unfortunate result of this is that people like Oum Mustafa save whatever spare cash they have in order to consult 'expert' private doctors when there is a serious illness. Some of these 'expert doctors' who prey on the poor have no medical qualifications or credentials apart from a brass plate inscribed with bogus qualifications. This adds a certain weight to Oum Mustafa's view that incorrect medical treatment caused her husband's death.

mad fury; I was horrified and outraged. Naturally it can
be explained by my lack of experience and knowledge of
the world outside the home. As Yussef's wife I had been
isolated from the hard facts of life. Everything had been
turned upside-down and my life had been thrown into a
turmoil. All the things I had been brought up to believe in
and the way of life I considered fine and honourable were
suddenly destroyed. Indeed, everything that I loved and
took pride in had gone forever.

I remember screaming at her, saying that I wasn't a
woman who would shame herself by working in the streets.
I reminded her that I had my honour, my respectable
status and good name to protect. I shouted all sorts of
things like that over and over. I'm ashamed to recall my
behaviour, I even told my sister that she was in no position
to advise me; had she ever lived a protected life, did she
know what it was like to be protected and cared for? I
can't be excused for saying such words, but you have to
understand my terror. I was like a lost child. For the first
time I had no man to provide for me and I hadn't come
to terms with my sister's plans for the future. But I'll never
forget her reaction, she just smiled sadly and said, 'Well so
be it, dear sister, I'll keep my mourning clothes ready for
you and your sons!'

Those words were like a bright, hot flame which burned
my flesh to the bone. I came to my senses at once and knew
that my sister had been right. We had to look after ourselves now that Yussef was gone. I had to earn money,
otherwise we would starve. All my sister's arrangements
were for the best. Unlike me, she'd known exactly what to
do because she'd been alone and penniless herself before
now. So there it was, my future was mapped out, and what
a future! But of course she was right and I still believe it,
even after all the hard work I've had to do, and getting
accustomed to a different way of life hasn't been easy!

In my heart I believe that women are not supposed to
work, their place is in their father's or husband's house.

A woman should only have to worry about domestic affairs and deal with cooking and cleaning and taking care of her husband and children. But when Yussef died I had young children to care for and a house to look after without a husband. As much as I hated the thought of work, I had to do it to feed my sons. I had to learn about men's affairs just to do my duty as a mother!

From that day on I never allowed myself to look back or doubt my ability to provide for our needs. My sister stayed on and she helps me a great deal with the children, the housework and the stall. I have the stall filled every day of the week. When I'm there my sister takes care of Mustafa and Hassim after school and prepares dinner. She also helps with a lot of the housework and shopping when I'm at work on the stall. It must sound a very unhappy life for my sons and myself, days filled with hard work and no play, but God has willed it this way and it must be so.

I am luckier than many women since we have the home Yussef provided, the means to earn money and the help of good neighbours. This makes me feel humble and grateful when I remember how proud and selfish I used to be. Many women without husbands have more problems than I do and I thank God for my good fortune in the last few years. It's not the life I would have chosen for myself, and God knows this is not how I lived in the past, but perhaps He desired that I see life from both sides.

I sell the very best produce I can find and restock my stall as often as possible. My stall! You see how those words slip out so easily, only a year ago I would have been embarrassed to admit that I ran a stall. At first I used Yussef's suppliers, who were very kind to me and gave me good advice when I started to work. But after some months my paternal cousin and I established a profitable agreement. Now he sends me the fruit he grows himself and I sell it. I make sure that he gets a fair price each season for his oranges or figs or whatever. It's a fair arrangement. Although he isn't a rich farmer he asks for little in return, but I always send him small gifts and more of a share of the profit than he asks for. You see, that's the importance of blood ties. These relationships work in a clever way; your kinsman does you a favour and asks for little in return, but he anticipates that you are so grateful for his assistance that you'll return twice as much as he requested in appreciation of his generosity!

The cousin I mentioned is a good man and the blood between us is strong and thick. But apart from kinship there is another explanation for his assistance. He is keeping this half-hidden at present because the desire is very close to his heart. Like most countrymen, he thinks that women are not very bright and don't understand plans and schemes! Of course we realised what he was after a long time ago. It's so obvious, he hopes to marry my sister, he admires her intelligence, strength and many other talents. He's not stupid, after all! Perhaps there will be a bond of marriage as well as blood between us before too long and then I will be really happy for my sister. I like to think that people who struggle against hardship are rewarded in the end. Maybe the marriage will be a gift as well as an extra bond between us, since it'll be a result of the hard times which brought us all together.

The small quantity of vegetables which I sell comes from another merchant in the city. He is a friend of my son-in-law, my elder daughter's good husband, so this all shows how you can never be truly alone as long as your family and friends are nurtured and thrive.

Despite what I've said about the stall, our money is never certain and I never take it for granted. Any day we might be penniless and have to eat dust. We live from day to day and any money which doesn't go for food gets saved for the future. I try to save whatever I can for the boys' education. I believe that going to school offers poor parents some hope that their children will make a better life for themselves. It's certainly one of my dearest wishes for my own children.

My older son Mustafa is a bright boy, wise beyond his years. He taught me a lot in the early days of my work and showed me just how ignorant I was. He had watched his father at the stall and picked up a lot of useful tips. The little one is very clever too and I know that he would do well in a job in an office. He could even get a position in the civil service or government administration, but that's probably just a mother's foolish dream. Still, like Mustafa, he is very bright and he really enjoys school. I will work my fingers to the bone to make sure that he can stay at school as long as he wants. I know Mustafa will run the stall when he's older, since he takes after Yussef and shows great skill at trading. His advice is very useful even now when he's still just a boy and can only work part-time because I insist that he finishes this year of school.

Most days I'm happy, but sometimes I wake up and think of the past. I find that there are days when I feel ashamed of working, despite everything I've said. It's hard for me to forget that I used to be a cherished wife who lived a life of honour and privilege. When I'm haunted by such memories it's difficult to face the day. I remember things too clearly, I suppose, and I'm still proud that I was a protected wife who didn't have to bother about the outside world.

Now I have to expose myself to life in the streets and often that involves seeing distasteful things. But on days like this my good sister's words start ringing in my ears. Then I try not to think of the past, I think of Mustafa and Hassim and it's impossible to forget my love and duty as a mother. Before long the feeling of sorrow and shame passes as I realise that this is how many women must live, and most of them have never had the blessing of life with a devoted husband.

As time passes I think that I can even see some honour in my work. I became a widow at quite a young age and work was forced on me by tragic circumstances. But I know that the stall is my only means of survival, feeding my children and providing for our needs.

If I have to earn money for my family like any man, it's clear that I'm a woman and a mother above everything else. Nobody would say that this isn't the case. My children and home life always come first! I'm a woman without a man, what's the alternative? There's no choice in such a situation. What woman would die because she was manless? What mother would rather bury her sons than overcome her fear of the outside world?

A serious difference of opinion had been brewing for several weeks between Oum Mustafa and the Sheikha, Oum Mohammed's closest friend. Angry words had been exchanged in public and this was followed by rumours that a final confrontation was imminent. All the women had their ears to the ground for further hints of the time and place of this exciting event. In the end, as everyone expected, the two wounded egos were salved and the matter of honour resolved, but no one anticipated the part that a tale would play in this. One fraught evening Oum Mustafa and the Sheikha were holding court on opposite sides of the tiny room when Oum Mohammed told the following tale.

THE SINGING BIRD

This is a tale about pride and foolishness. It tells of a happy captivity and an unhappy liberty. What is the difference? Which is the best? Like all opposites, like two sides of the same coin, these things don't mix well and can't exist side by side, except of course in a tale.

Once there was a very rich man who lived in a very fine house. He had many splendid things but there was one he loved with all his heart and he valued it over everything else. The man had a beautiful songbird which he kept in a silver cage. This was his most prized possession. The bird had rich feathers of blue and green and gold, but even more beautiful than its feathers was its beautiful voice. The bird could have enchanted demons with this voice, and indeed the man's ugly moods always disappeared when the bird started to sing. The man was so proud of his bird that he never stopped talking about it. He liked to invite all his friends home and entertain them lavishly, then he would set the songbird's cage in the centre of the table and ask it to sing. True to tell, the man's guests were never bored however many times this happened. The bird sang so beautifully that it even drove away feelings of envy and jealousy which might have accompanied the guests' admiration.

Although the man was very wealthy and successful he was also lonely. He had no children to lighten his heart and his friends sometimes seemed more interested in his money than in him. Because of this sad situation he invested all his love in the songbird. He would spend every evening at home with the bird, talking to it as if it was his dearest companion. The man would tell the bird his secrets, reveal his fears and explain his plans for the future. In response, the bird sang to him to soothe his cares and worries and celebrate his successes. The beautiful bird knew songs which suited every human emotion and everyone who heard it sing claimed that its beautiful voice had expressed the exact emotion they were feeling.

The less prosperous people of the neighbourhood were always finding some excuse to stand near the wealthy man's house in the hope of hearing the beautiful songbird. Some would loiter on the pavement underneath the window, others would sit on the wall at the front of the house. The poor people loved to hear the songbird although, of course, the man did not approve. The man was more vigilant in the care of his fine songbird than a father jealously guarding his unmarried daughter. He often rushed outside and chased the miserable people away with a string of abusive comments. Sometimes he told them to mind their own business and go back to their hovels. At other times he would accuse them of wanting to steal the bird and call them thieves and cheats. He usually ended this abuse of his poor neighbours with the rude suggestion that they should work harder in order to buy a songbird of their own. In fact the owner of the beautiful songbird was not a very nice man because he was sad and lonely, or perhaps he was sad and lonely because he was not a nice man! The beautiful songbird sat inside the house in its silver cage and waited for the man to stop chasing the neighbours away. When the man came in hot and bothered it would sing a sweet song and all would be well again.

The songbird did nothing all day when the man was at work which did not reflect the fact of his absence. It preened and washed its fine feathers to make sure that they would glisten when the man returned. It rested its fine voice to make sure that it would be perfectly tuned to greet the man when he crossed the threshold. The bird checked that its fine bell was working so that it would tinkle and chime to accompany its singing if the man so desired. These important tasks kept it occupied all day and not for one moment was it ever bored in its fine silver cage. The man had hung a little silver mirror framed with gold in the cage. On the rare occasions when the beautiful songbird finished preening and resting and tinkling its bell before the man returned, it spent the rest of the afternoon just gazing happily at its own image in the glass.

The songbird could not look after its own cage, of course. The man paid a local woman to do his daily chores and prepare his evening meal. This servant also had to clean and polish the beautiful songbird's beautiful cage.

The bird watched as the woman swept the floor and dusted the man's furniture. It watched while the rugs were beaten and the dishes were washed and the meals were prepared. The bird never missed anything and it always noticed if the woman neglected to sweep out the kitchen or air the washing before putting it away. When the chores were finished she turned her attention to the silver cage. This was the task she always left to the last since she enjoyed cleaning the cage most of all. Although she was poor, she found pleasure, like most poor people, in touching any beautiful thing which she could never have afforded for herself. But she also liked polishing the cage because it was not tiring and made few demands on her worn-out body. The fine songbird felt proud when the woman stared at the silver cage in wonder, but it did not like her at all. When she started to wipe dust from the bars of the cage it was bumped about and sometimes thrown from its perch. The bird was sure that the woman was deliberately clumsy in order to upset it.

Each day when the cleaning woman had finished her work the songbird sat happily in its beautiful cage looking out through the shining bars. This is my whole world, thought the bird in delight. The songbird thought that it was perfect to be so safe and well cared for and adored. Sometimes it would look out of the window and watch other less talented, less beautiful birds. How pathetic they are, it thought. The songbird always felt superior as it observed how these birds squabbled and fought while they searched for food scraps outside in the dangerous streets.

Once a great bird of prey was seen in the neighbourhood. Many people gathered to watch it soar and dive above the roof-tops in the square. It was huge and when it spread its wings they were several feet wide. The beautiful songbird was fascinated, it had never seen such magnificent wings before, nor such graceful flight. In fact it had never flown at all as there was hardly room to stretch its wings in the cage. Anyway, what need was there to fly? The songbird watched the great bird which was attracting so much attention and grew annoyed. What was so interesting about it apart from its size? It had no fine voice or fine cage, all it did was swoop and soar. Surely the people were wasting their time staring at this big bird? Couldn't they see that it was of no importance? If it was so attractive a bird why did nobody want to put it in a silver cage and care for it? The beautiful songbird felt better thinking how tough the great bird's life must be. The songbird was glad that it didn't have to hunt for food and struggle for survival like the bird of prey.

One day the songbird was admiring itself in the little mirror, waiting for the man to return, when it noticed a nasty mean-looking cat on the window ledge. The cat stared at the bird with hungry eyes, and prowled across the window ledge until it was right in front of the cage. It did not take its eyes off the bird for a moment. Although it could not reach the cage, the hungry cat enjoyed alarming the beautiful songbird behind the silver bars. After a while the bird realised that the cat represented no real threat and it was in no danger. The cat could only stare with those mean and hungry eyes. The songbird forgot its fear and began to mock the cat. It hopped about the cage to tease the cat, secure in the knowledge that it could come to no harm inside its fine cage. It laughed at the cat in its superior fashion. Nobody cared for the cat, it was all alone in the world and too ugly to attract admiring glances and flattering words.

One evening the owner of the songbird invited a great number of important guests to his home. His servant prepared a splendid feast and after the meal, as usual, the songbird's cage was uncovered and it sang to entertain the guests. These important men adored the bird. They praised its beautiful voice, they admired its beautiful plumage, they said how much they desired to own such a bird, although of course they said that they would never find one which was as wonderful as their host's. The bird understood everything that the men said since it had been in the constant company of humans all its life. In fact it had ceased to consider itself a bird and had forgotten that most birds do not have an easy protected life in a silver cage.

The songbird sang for the men again and again, never tiring of their sweet words and delighting in the titbits they offered as reward. When everyone had gone home at last, the owner of this beautiful bird grew melancholy and

thoughtful, all alone again with his most valued possession. He gazed at the songbird fondly and begged it never
to leave him. He said all manner of foolish things. He
asked if the bird loved him more than anything else in the
world. He asked it to promise never to fly away. Of course
the bird could not respond in human speech, but it was
thrilled with these signs of devotion and sang the most
beautiful melodies it knew to please the man.

The beautiful songbird only knew adoration, flattery
and praise. When the man left the house the bird waited
impatiently for his return. The cleaning woman did not
pay it much attention on her daily visits except to check
that it had water and bird-seed and to polish the silver cage.

One day the woman arrived with her young son. The
bird did not know that the little boy had been begging his
mother to take him to see the beautiful songbird for many
months. Of course if the bird had known this it would not
have been so irritated by the child's unexpected appearance. The beautiful bird was annoyed by any interruption
to its day-long preparations for the man's return. How
could it preen and stare at its fine reflection and not be
disturbed by this nosy child?

The little boy peered into the cage and urged the bird
to sing. He told the bird that it was the most beautiful bird
in the world, but the songbird was accustomed to more
elaborate praise from more important people. The beautiful bird would not sing. Why should it bother! It was
further annoyed by the child's stupidity. Didn't this urchin
know that it never sang during the day? Didn't the brat
understand that the fine voice had to be rested? What
annoyed the fine bird most was the child's presumption.
It certainly wouldn't sing for such a poor, ill-dressed,
uninvited guest in its master's own home! The child was
disappointed that he did not hear the bird's beautiful
voice. He rattled the cage and tapped the bars trying to
force a note or two from the silent bird's beak. The bird
was furious and flapped and screeched until the woman

dragged the child away and scolded him. The beautiful
songbird wished that it had had a chance to peck at this
hateful boy. It was delighted when the mother and child
left the house. The fine bird did not know that one day that
little boy would play a major part in changing its life.

 Some time later there was a terrible tragedy which
shocked everyone in the neighbourhood. The songbird
was puzzled and confused. All at once its secure routine
was disrupted. Nothing made sense. The man had not
come home, although the bird waited and waited for
the sound of his footsteps. There had been no guests in the
house, even the cleaning woman had not appeared. The
bird was hungry and afraid and lonely until the day of
a funeral when it understood that a terrible thing had
happened. The wealthy man who owned many fine things,
the finest being the beautiful songbird, had been killed in
an accident.

 There was a big expensive funeral attended by many
colleagues, employees and those people the man had called
his friends. Suddenly the man's home was filled with
people who fought over the right to take possession of
his fine furnishings, his ornaments, his rugs and his
silver. The greedy crowd was only interested in the most
valuable things which they could sell. They all agreed that
the songbird was a wonder but that it was unlikely to fetch
much money in the market place. Everyone was too busy
filling their bags with the dead man's possessions to give
a second thought to the bird. They had no time for com-
pliments and sweet words, indeed they ignored the bird
completely. The bird was terrified as it gradually realised
that its former life had come to an end. Never again would
it swell with pride at its master's adoring glances. It began
to screech, it was hungry, afraid and neglected. For the
first time it heard people tell it to shut up. The beautiful
songbird was outraged and vowed never to sing again.

 The only person who bothered about the songbird was
the cleaning woman. She came back to the empty house,

stripped bare by the man's greedy friends, lifted the cage and carried it off. In the woman's home the bird looked at its new surroundings in horror. There were no fine things, just a poor woman's worn-out furnishings. Her children gathered around the cage in delight and stared at the bird. They all urged it to sing, the youngest boy louder than the rest. The bird remembered this child with disgust. It sat on its perch and regarded them defiantly. The songbird which had vowed not to sing found some small comfort in observing the children's disappointment. But before long they grew bored and left the bird alone. After all, what use is a songbird that doesn't sing?

Although the cleaning women's children were fed up with the bird's stubborn silence, her little son persisted in asking it to sing. He sat by the cage every morning and whispered kind things and told the bird not to feel lonely and sad. The boy brought different things for the bird to eat and began to polish its cage, but the songbird continued to ignore him. It began to hate the child and his weak attempts at flattery. The bird especially hated the boy when he urged it to cheer up.

One day the child was coaxing the bird to sing, feeding it the nuts his mother could ill afford, and rubbing his fingers along the bars of the fine cage. The songbird tried not to listen to the little boy but could not shut out the childish words of pity. The bird was never comforted by the child's efforts, being too proud of its fine past to appreciate this lesser show of appreciation. In a sudden show of bad temper, the bird snapped at the child and gave his finger a vicious peck. The child screamed with pain and shock, fell off the chair and knocked the cage over.

The songbird crashed to the floor inside its cage. The fine silver hinge on the cage door was smashed, and as the bird flapped its wings in terror it found itself flying across the room and out of the window. The bird landed on the uppermost branch of the tree in the square without know-ing how this happened. It looked from side to side and up and down, but where was its fine cage? Where were the shining bars of silver? The beautiful bird was outside, unprotected and alone. The songbird was stunned. It did not dare to move. It did not know how it had reached this branch. It did not know how to fly again. In fact it knew nothing except that it was certain to perish.

When the songbird looked down it saw other birds perching on the lower branches. These birds were neither beautiful nor talented. They had very ordinary singing voices and the songbird could not think why they bothered to burst into song so often. It watched and wondered at their behaviour. Wasn't it pitiable they way they eagerly went off in search of food but only found food scraps from the dump? The songbird was weak with hunger but nobody came with bird-seed. The other birds were too busy to pay much attention to the isolated newcomer. They did not attempt to befriend it, remembering how it used to mock them. The songbird did not approach them because it was still unaware that it too was a bird, outside in the world that most birds inhabit. The fine cage and the doting master were long gone.

As time passed the songbird learned a few things about its new world. It was able to fly after the other birds when they searched for scraps. It realised that the dump was the best place to find food. It survived with luck and discovered useful things by accident and trial and error. The existence of dangerous enemies was one shocking discovery. In the safety of its silver cage the songbird had not guessed that the world was such a terrible place. The hungry-eyed cat was the worst enemy of all. The cat hunted all the birds but was especially keen to capture the beautiful songbird. Day after day the songbird lived in terror of the cat, and many times just managed to evade its cruel claws.

One day the songbird was perched on a low branch staring at the window of its former fine home. It dreamed of the past and was full of self-pity. Suddenly it was in the cat's mouth, frantically struggling against the sharp teeth which gripped its beautiful tail feathers. Other birds watched from higher, safer branches as the songbird fought to get free. At the very last moment the songbird flapped away, leaving most of its fine tail in the cat's mouth. The other birds flew down in excitement and the terrified songbird found itself surrounded by the flock for the very first time. The other birds rejoiced at the songbird's lucky victory over their common enemy. The songbird was shaken and weak but not badly hurt, although nobody would call it beautiful again.

After this the songbird made some friends in the community of birds, but it was still rather distant and aloof. It knew that it faced the same hardship as the others, but the memory of past splendour, flattery and devotion made the songbird feel superior to them. The other birds sensed this and did not challenge the songbird's foolish notion. They were a little sorry that the songbird still had many hard lessons to learn and even came to pity it for its easy life in the silver cage. Clearly this was the cause of its problems. The other birds knew that the songbird's pride and foolishness were born of ignorance and luxury, although they had once envied its life of ease.

Winter was on its way and the nights were growing colder. The birds struggled to build up a store of food for the hard season ahead. One day another newcomer arrived in the tree. It was a tiny, care-worn bird which had flown for hundreds of miles in search of its mate. The pair had been separated months before during a storm. The poor bird was exhausted and near to death. This was not unusual and the story did not stir the other bird's hearts. Hardship and trouble and sudden death were a familiar part of their everyday life. The birds were accustomed to sad stories, they had seen many of their fellows die in similar sad situations. The tiny bird sat alone while the flock flew off in search of food for their own families. It simply waited for death and knew that the others had to take care of themselves.

The songbird had been listening from its nest below. It was moved to pity by the tiny bird's story, remembering its own loss and being less hardened to sorrow than the others. The songbird was not aware how the life of sudden hardship had changed it for the better. In the days of the silver cage it would have been too selfish to feel pity for a pathetic bird at the mercy of fate. So, when the other birds disappeared from view, the songbird joined the tiny one on the branch where it had been abandoned. It could see that it was very weak, and dying of starvation and exhaustion. The songbird returned to its nest and began to bring scraps from its winter store to the tiny bird, and it did not rest until the tiny bird had finished all the food and was showing signs of recovery.

That night when the others returned they were astonished to see the songbird and the newcomer sharing the same nest. This was the act that finally changed the songbird's life. It was a more important event than that evening when the man's most honoured guests had proclaimed it the sweetest singer in the world. It was of greater significance than the man's death or the child's accident which had broken the silver cage. Of all the things that the songbird had learned, and all the things that it had done, this unselfish act towards a fellow creature confirmed its place in the world of birds. The songbird and its tiny companion became close friends and allies, each one grateful for mutual kindnesses and the chance of a new life.

One morning when winter had passed the songbird looked out of its nest to the square below. It had been a cold winter and food had been scarce. The songbird had often been hungry, but it had never once regretted using the store of food to save the tiny bird. Now that the days were warmer it was easier to find food and life was becoming more pleasant. The songbird was filled with happiness, grateful just to have survived to feel the warm sun again. At last it realised that life outside the cage was often unpleasant and never easy, but the important thing was that it was no man's possession. It could fly when and where it chose. It could sing, not for praise but for joy if it so desired. The songbird spread its wings and suddenly burst into a fine song to greet the spring.

The tale's triumphant conclusion was greeted with cheers. Everyone tried to do the impossible — to flatter the storyteller and not go cross-eyed trying to see both Oum Mustafa's and the Sheikha's reaction at the same time. The two women had not moved from their original positions. They remained in opposite corners of the room, no more than a few metres apart, but they could well have been on different planets. Oum Mustafa was the first to speak. She said that it was a very good tale. The Sheikha immediately added that she also thought it was a very good tale, and a very moral one. Oum Mustafa was quick to reply that the best part was the ending; the conclusion was the most important part. After a difficult pause, the Sheikha agreed with her, then they both emphasised that it was a very good tale from start to finish. This seemed enough to satisfy honour on both sides, and the two women had established a cool but polite truce before the final round of cakes was finished.

The other women were eager to discuss the tale's effect on Oum Mustafa and her disagreement with the Sheikha. The general consensus was that Oum Mohammed's ingenuity had been underestimated once again. A storyteller's wily diplomacy never failed to thrill the audience. Oum Idris' comment caught the spirit of the evening when she said that a good tale had more than one meaning and involved more than just smart words.

Wily diplomacy and smart words were phrases which were foremost in my mind throughout my last evening in the neighbourhood. My imminent departure was the perfect excuse for a party. There was an emotional ambivalence to the occasion, but we were determined to forget the tearful goodbyes which were bound to come the following morning. Oum Idris was brimming over with wicked jokes at my expense and made a point of mimicking my faulty Arabic every time she spoke. Gifts were exchanged and examined with great interest on both sides. I was surrounded by every child in the room, being the recipient of several kilos of sweets. There was a semblance of anarchy as a huge amount of party food appeared. Oum Mohammed called for silence and tried to establish some order, without notable success, and the noise did not subside until Oum Mustafa horrified me by calling for a speech.

It was a very unimpressive speech. I had very little to say on the spur of the moment and soon dried up, being deserted by anything that might pass for wit, wisdom or eloquence. The women all roared with laughter. 'Tell us your life story instead,' someone shouted. 'You must have learned *something* from us by now!' More laughter. To my relief the children were spotted making off with my pile of sweets, and chaos broke out again. More tea and cakes were needed before general conversation could be resumed. Everyone was talking at once and I was trying to take part in several conversations at the same time. The women dredged up their favourite questions from my first months in the neighbourhood. This time they were asked with the advantage of hindsight: What had I *really* been doing? Why had I wanted then to talk about their lives? Why was I so nosy? Was there anything else I wanted to know? Why had I never asked about really interesting things?

I made a final attempt to answer their questions. After so much practice perhaps I would manage to find some adequate explanations at the eleventh hour and make up for my earlier disaster with the farewell speech. I talked about the life stories and my interest in their view of their world, which was so different from my own. I said I felt privileged to have shared something of their world, and to have heard about their lives. I explained that I had learned lots of things which I could put in the book I wanted to write about them. I felt quite pleased with this but although there were a few nods of appreciation nobody seemed very impressed with my fine words. I must have looked disheartened and embarrassed again because everyone laughed. 'What about the tales?' asked Oum Mohammed.

I saw that Oum Mustafa and the Sheikha were also watching me intently. 'Well, I loved the tales,' I said. 'Did you listen to them properly?' Now the Sheikha had me transfixed with her steely stare. I replied cautiously that I'd always listened carefully as the storyteller demanded. The Sheikha was determined to get a better answer than that: 'Did you listen properly and understand the tales?' I took a deep breath and tried not to panic.

'Well,' I said, scanning Amira's face for inspiration, 'I always listened very carefully and I think that I always understood the storyteller's meaning.' I wanted to stop before I said something particularly foolish which might cause offence but now Oum Mustafa joined the inquistion. 'Did you understand everything in every tale?' she demanded. I said that this was a very difficult question because there must have been a lot of minor details which went over my head. And of course the tales were so clever and complex that I couldn't have understood everything. 'Did you understand enough?' the Sheikha asked. I could see that everyone was watching me now, waiting for my reply. 'Of course I understood enough, more than enough,' I said in what I hoped was my most confident voice. 'Good!' said Oum Mohammed.

There was a widespead nodding of heads and approving noises. Someone broke the silence which followed with a call for a tale. Oum Mohammed narrowed her eyes and flashed me an unexpected wink: 'Now listen hard and be sure to understand every word *this* time!'

THE TALE OF THE HONEY BEE

This is the tale of a honey bee and it isn't an epic tale or a splendid romance. The tale isn't very long or romantic or mysterious because this wouldn't suit the honey bee at all! It is a tale about trial and error and about knowing when enough is enough. It's also a bit of a comic tale because, unlike mystery and romance, a joke always suits the honey bee.

Once upon a time there was a honey bee which landed in a strange new garden. How it got there was a matter of some speculation. The general opinion was that the honey bee had ended up in the garden by accident. The honey bee seemed to attract accidents and daft mistakes. It was that kind of bee! The other inhabitants of the garden thought that it had lost its way. Some said that it had fallen out of a passing plane. Others said that a freak wind had blown it off-course. The rest had no idea at all, but were sure that some kind of accident had brought the bee to their garden.

What the honey bee was actually doing was the cause of much speculation too. There was nothing about the bee which made much sense at all. It wås a mystery, a puzzle, a curiosity! Some said that the bee was simply deranged and this explained its curious ways. Others said that although it looked a lot like a bee, it wasn't a bee at all and this explained why it behaved in a most un-beelike manner. The rest had no explanation for its activities; it did curious things because it was a curious bee, no more and no less than that! Certainly it was a very peculiar kind of bee with all kinds of peculiar habits and interests. It worked very hard, this was clear to everyone, but it seemed to like exhausting itself performing the strangest tasks. Of course there were the accidents and daft mistakes as well. It was that kind of bee!

The honey bee rose early every morning and went to bed late at night. This is the first peculiar habit people noticed. Of course this meant that it was always very tired, but although there was an obvious remedy for the situation, it refused to change its sleeping habits. It was that kind of bee!

The honey bee liked to talk a lot. Not in the ordinary sense, of course. It always wanted to discuss the most peculiar things. This was the second strange habit that people noticed. The bee didn't seem content to talk about anything sensible like clothes and movies and food. Oh no, it was only interested in talking about boring subjects and it loved to ask questions about the most obvious things.

If someone was eating breakfast you could be sure that the honey bee would appear and ask why the person was eating and what hunger felt like. If someone was fast asleep the honey bee would make a point of waking them up to ask what it was like to sleep. If someone told a great joke the honey bee would laugh and laugh with everyone else and then ask why it was funny. Indeed, even if the honey bee was invited to a wedding it wouldn't dream of having a good time at the feast like everyone else. Oh no, it went around asking who had married whom, and why, and what marriage was.

The honey bee worked very hard and was totally mad about work. This was another daft thing about the honey bee. Naturally it had very strange working habits, and of course it did nothing that looked like work to anyone else. It was fascinated with the subject of work and since it liked to talk so much and ask questions, work was one of its favourite topics. It asked the most ridiculous questions you ever heard: 'Do you work? What is work? What do you think about working?' It had at least a hundred different ways of asking the same questions and never seemed to tire of them. It seemed to love hearing the same answers over and over again as well. The bee was even heard to ask people if they liked work. What a question! But you have to remember that it was that kind of bee. Peculiar!

The activities which the bee called work were a cause of much speculation. What was it doing? Why? For what reason? These were the questions which people asked. In fact, some of the time it seemed as if the honey bee's habit of asking endless questions was infectious! Honey bees are busy by nature and this one was no exception. What was peculiar was how it kept busy. Honey bees collect honey and that's that, just honey, no more and no less! But this honey bee was not *that* kind of bee! This peculiar honey bee was happy to collect anything at all. Sometimes it found honey and sometimes it found worms. Both times it was equally happy. It seemed to think that collecting things was the important part of its work, and that what it collected didn't matter. This was another curious habit which intrigued its friends.

The honey bee delighted in its work, which was another strange thing people noticed about it. It worked from dawn to dusk and moved at such a speed that it left a dust trail behind it. People got so used to this whirlwind of activity that after a while when they saw a cloud of dust on the horizon they simply said there goes that bee again and thought nothing more about it. When the bee set out to find honey it did so in a very peculiar fashion. It did not have the regular, methodical approach common to most honey bees. It appeared to be somewhat confused about the best sources of honey. Sometimes it didn't even seem to know what honey was!

All the same, it must be said that the honey bee worked very hard and it always enjoyed itself. Day after day it was seen flitting from flower to flower. It was keen to collect as much honey as possible but of course it often looked in the strangest places. Of course it visited petals and flowering shrubs, the expected sources of honey. However, there were other occasions when the bee was seen to land on dung heaps and tin cans as if it thought the best honey of all was to be found there. People tried to tell it that these were unlikely honey pots, but this didn't diminish its determination. It had faith in its own daft ways. It was that kind of bee!

The honey bee also looked a little strange, not at all as you'd expect. People are used to seeing sweet little honey bees, round and fluffy and plump little honey bees, but they had never seen one like this before. The honey bee that couldn't tell the difference between a petal and a dung heap had a similar problem with its looks: it couldn't tell the difference between hair oil and glue. As a result it had astonishing spiky hair instead of the usual soft fluffy look of a honey bee.

People tried to help because the bee had many well meaning friends. But, sad to say, it went through numerous beautifying processes without any successful results. These efforts were hopeless but the honey bee didn't seem to mind. It was that kind of bee!

When people teased it and made jokes, which was most of the time, the honey bee laughed too. But once when its friends had spent all evening trying to make it soft and fluffy the bee grew impatient and a little cross. 'Why bother! It's a waste of time!' it snapped, and it struggled to get away from the beauty products. As fate would have it, this was the one time that its friends had almost succeeded in making it look like a bee should look. But of course the cross honey bee immediately fell into a puddle and became spiky and untidy again. * Everyone laughed and the bee stopped being cross. It was that kind of bee!

The honey bee did other very odd things which nobody could understand. While it loved to talk and talk and talk, it also loved to be alone. Sometimes it was seen sitting quite apart from everyone else. Because it was a most strange bee it didn't simply sit in silence, which might make sense when you think how talkative it was. Oh no, this bee often sat quite alone and buzzed and hummed and chattered to itself with a far-away look in its eyes. At first people used to worry that it might be quite mad, but in time they realised that it wasn't completely crazy, but only a little strange! In fact the honey bee was like a radio which was never switched off!† The bee always had to be surrounded by voices and it didn't seem to matter whose voices they were or whether they were talking sense or not.

During the long summer the bee's collection grew and grew. Its stores grew bigger and bigger. Something had to be done about this! There was hardly any room left for the

---

* During fieldwork many friends devoted themselves to the cause of improving my looks with a consistent lack of success. Hairdressing was a particular interest. One attempt to oil and curl my hair until it looked like local women's thick glossy tresses ended with an accident similar to the honey bee's. I grew impatient and rather irritated after several hours of hairdressing, and refused to wait until the process was completed, despite repeated warnings. The wax which had been combed through my hair hardened in the heat and much to everyone's amusement I was left with hair which looked as if it was made of plastic and stood on end for weeks.

† People used to tease me about my continual use of a tape recorder, particularly when I played the tapes back late at night and the sound of different well known voices was heard coming from my room. One running joke was that I was a one-woman radio station broadcasting twenty-four hours a day.

honey bee in its tiny home, which was stuffed with supplies. The room wasn't the only thing to be full to burst-
ing point. The honey bee was so full of the things it had
collected that it could hardly move. It was stuffed full of
honey. It was fat and growing fatter every day. It was
quite the fattest bee imaginable, although you wouldn't
have noticed it. The fattest bee in the world was fat in a
peculiar way of course.* It was that kind of bee!

However, when the summer was over the honey bee
started to think about returning to its real home, wherever
that was! It went searching for new things to collect at an
even faster speed than usual. The honey bee knew that it
had to return to its own family to make good use of the
things it had found in the garden. True to tell it began to
behave in an even stranger manner. It started to collect
anything it could find and the pile of supplies grew bigger
and bigger. The bee was delighted to carry off whatever
it found, whether it was honey or whether it was rubbish.
It was soon sleeping outside because it had given its bed
over to the collection of junk.

Finally, the morning of the honey bee's departure had
come. Everyone was sad because, of course, it was a very
sad day. The garden would seem very empty without
the honey bee's continual chatter and questions. For once
it was not rushing around, but standing quietly with its
friends. The honey bee was surrounded by all the things
it had collected during its visit. There were boxes and bags
filled with honey and all sorts of junk and the bee itself was
fatter than ever. It was a very different bee from the nervous little creature which had first arrived in the garden.

---

* This reference to the bee's 'peculiar kind of fatness' produced loud laughter.
By local standards I was judged pitifully thin with a miserable figure. Women
said that this explained why I wasn't married, and they found my utter dislike
of their favourite dishes very amusing. Another joke at my expense was that
my brain used up all the food I ate and left nothing for my flesh. People said
that I should spend less time thinking and asking questions if I didn't want
to disappear completely.

While it was a sad day, a very sad day indeed, everyone knew that the honey bee had to go back to its own family. The friends were all embracing and wishing each other good luck and a happy life. They hoped that the honey bee would find itself a mate as soon as it returned home and they joked and teased it as usual, although they were just as sad as the honey bee. They all said that they would always remember its visit, which is true enough and not at all surprising! The most important thing was that everybody had a great store of memories to comfort them in the future and of course they would never forget each other.

Of course the peculiar life in the garden had to come to an end because this was the right time for the honey bee to go home. For one thing, it couldn't stay any longer because its family were waiting for it. For another thing, it would have to walk home if its collection got any bigger, or even worse, it would burst if it got any fatter!

The tale had been subject to constant interruption by ribald comments and in-jokes and continual laughter, but now there was relative quiet. I looked round the room and raised my eyebrows and smiled. I was determined not to be the first to break the silence or comment on the tale. I looked from Amira to Oum Karim to Oum Sherif and Oum Ali and back to Amira. Their expressions seemed inscrutable. I didn't dare to search for clues in any of the storytellers' faces, and was particularly keen to avoid catching Oum Mohammed's eye. Finally I turned to Oum Idris and we were overcome by a fit of childish giggles. 'Did you understand every word? Did you grasp the meaning?' she asked in an excellent daring impersonation of Oum Mohammed's rather abrupt manner. But by this stage our laughter had infected everybody else and I was incapable of speech.

The party continued for another few hours, and family dinners were postponed or abandoned that night. Before I left I thanked the storyteller again and heaped praise on her for the clever tale which had caused so much mirth. 'And you understood the meaning of every word as usual!' It was not a question this time. Oum Mohammed could never resist having the final word. But I had learned a little about smart words and wily diplomacy myself. 'It was a wonderful tale,' I repeated, having flattered her several times already, 'I understood every word but I'm not certain of the meaning. These clever tales have so many meanings.'